TOO CONSCIOUS FOR THIS WORLD

Too Conscious for This World

You're Not Wrong. You're Early.

By Candace van Dell

©2026 All Rights Reserved. No portion of this book may be reproduced, stored in a retrieval system, or transmitted in any form or by any means—electronic, mechanical, photocopy, recording, scanning, or other—except for brief quotations in critical reviews or articles without the prior permission of the author.

Published by Game Changer Publishing

Paperback ISBN: 979-8-90158-218-3
Hardcover ISBN: 979-8-90158-175-9
Digital ISBN: 979-8-90158-176-6

www.GameChangerPublishing.com

DEDICATION

To the ones who see beyond the illusion,

who were never able to fully subscribe to the matrix as it was presented to them—

You are not here to fit in but to elevate.

You are here to see clearly, to question boldly, and to transform what others blindly accept.

You were born different to make a difference.

There is nothing to fix, but something to trust.

There is nothing wrong with you.

You simply see what's wrong in the very world you were raised in—

and you have the courage to feel it, name it, and disrupt it.

You were not born on the wrong planet; you were born to shift the way of the world.

This is not a flaw.

It is intelligence.

It is your soul refusing to forget.

You didn't come here to belong to the world as it is.

You came here to change it simply by expressing your authenticity.

You are not behind.

You are not broken.

You are early.

You were born perfect for your divine purpose.

Read This First

Just to say thanks for buying and reading my book, I would like to offer some more helpful tools!

Scan the QR Code here.

TOO CONSCIOUS FOR THIS WORLD

YOU'RE NOT WRONG. YOU'RE EARLY.

CANDACE VAN DELL

TABLE OF CONTENTS

INTRODUCTION

"You are not wrong. You are early in a world that does not yet have a mirror for your level of consciousness."

There's nothing wrong with you. Being a highly sensitive soul in an emotional dark age is deeply challenging.

My name is Candace van Dell, and I have been working as a spiritual coach and teacher for the past thirteen years. My professional journey began when I was studying for my master's in Spiritual Psychology. I started posting videos on YouTube about my own insights that gave birth to my own healing modalities. I did not expect anyone to follow; I did it as a form of self-validation. To my surprise, within the first week, I grew to over ten thousand subscribers. Eventually, it became over one hundred thousand subscribers and many millions of views. By talking about my own processes and guiding others, I connected with many who were walking a similar yet unique path home to self. This was the place they would truly feel seen and deeply understood.

Over time, it evolved into a podcast and a dozen online courses. I formed my Truth Room membership so that highly sensitive, neurodivergent, and awakening people could connect around the world. This is all aimed at helping truth seekers globally who are seeking to truly heal and embrace their authentic selves and higher purposes. The Truth Room and my courses became a soul school of their own. The belonging you never had but always wanted. The mirror you never saw but finally found.

In this book, I continue that mission, explaining why you may feel scapegoated by a world or family system that minimizes your sensitivities and how to empower yourself to become the conscious leader you were always meant to be. This journey will help you break generational cycles and align with your higher purpose, ushering in a new consciousness.

You were born different for a reason: to make a difference. You are a disruptor of an outdated system, born to lead the way to a new paradigm. But first, you must heal the shame of never belonging, feeling abandoned, and ultimately self-abandoning. I'll discuss the rise of diagnoses and labels like ADHD (Attention Deficit Hyperactivity Disorder). I often refer to this as "Attention Dialed to a Higher Dimension" and "neurodivergence," both of which have skyrocketed since my own diagnosis in 1985.

Society tends to label and reject what it doesn't understand, but it's essential to own your differences to truly make a difference. I will share insights on how to heal the unhealed empath and help you make sense of expressing your truth in a world that often cannot hear it. You will learn about your powerful purpose as a sensitive person in a reality that lacks emotional intelligence.

This world is in a period that I call an "emotional dark age," thriving on denial rather than on the truth. It's not anyone's fault;

it's simply part of our evolution. But the paradigm is shifting, and we are being asked to rise as heart-centered leaders.

Understanding how your parents and their parents were raised sheds light on the generational trauma you came here to break. Though it is not their fault that they were wounded, it was their responsibility to become emotionally aware and not project their issues onto you.

As a sensitive soul, I was always seeking a deeper understanding. When I had my spiritual awakening at sixteen, I lacked a mirror for my experience, which threw me into an existential crisis. I had no choice but to seek out spiritual law and immerse myself in decades of inner work.

Being a highly sensitive person in an emotionally dark age meant that my experiences were often invalidated. Traditional therapy never reached the root of the issue, and spiritual psychology did not yet exist. My emotions felt invalidated, and I struggled to feel valid.

I wandered with an uncertain identity, determined to uncover the missing piece. I went through significant suffering as a young person, facing challenges like self-abandonment, self-sabotage, self-doubt, and perfectionism.

I felt disconnected and frustrated with both God and life. Yet, at the same time, my awakening began to restore my deep connection to my instincts, intuition, and insight. I found myself caught between a world of pain and one of profound insight.

I believe that my journey into many different types of healing modalities and spiritual teachings has shaped the wisdom underlying my work. It was incredibly confusing to experience intense emotions and spiritual insights without the language to express them or anyone to relate to. Imagine the turmoil of having your feelings and insights heightened while being trapped in a system that aims to break you down.

I often felt lost and out of control. I questioned where God was and why society seemed so misguided. I wondered why I always felt like an orphan when I clearly wasn't. Doubt crept into my mind about my perceptions and emotional truths, but somehow I held on to the inner guidance that kept drawing me forward.

An unhealed empath tends to take on the emotional burdens of others, attempting to help or "fix" them in hopes of feeling better in their own environments. This dynamic, which I refer to as "energetic codependency," often results in true feelings being scapegoated, especially in unconscious places dominated by family members who deny their own trauma.

Society, too, scapegoats us when we question the prevailing narrative. When we try to express our authentic selves, we may face punishment for our honesty. Over time, we might internalize these reactions or resort to coping mechanisms for relief. Many sensitive people I work with have felt a deep fear that they would be burned at the stake for telling the truth.

Both scenarios lead to a level of self-abandonment and a disconnection from our true emotions. This disconnection alienates us from our inner child and erodes our confidence, causing us to seek validation externally and depend on unreliable people.

This is how we attract toxic relationships and unavailable partners, perpetuating cycles that distance us from our authentic selves. We keep seeking external validation and identity, hoping for reassurance that it is safe to embrace our worth. Often, this affirmation never comes because we have been living in the collective unconscious.

We begin to see society as a false idol, praying to others' opinions while striving to meet their expectations and constantly searching for a "permission slip" to align with ourselves. We walk around with uncertain identities, trading our true selves for idealized versions to survive.

As a highly sensitive person often scapegoated by family and society, you may spend years searching for your true tribe. Everything changes when you have the courage to embrace your emotional honesty. You resurrect your authentic self by being truthful about your feelings, enabling your healing process.

This shadow work involves becoming unapologetically honest about your emotions, rejecting their rejection, and transforming your role from scapegoat to cycle breaker. As you develop a deeper understanding of yourself, your internal identity evolves, and your purpose becomes clearer.

When you align your actions with your own perspective, you become an undeniable force. Your integrity creates an impact, and your family may shift around your newfound identity or remain in their false reality. Ultimately, you have the opportunity to live the life you were born to lead, serving a purpose that elevates the world.

This is my story, as well as the story of hundreds of thousands of others I have been fortunate to work with. I hope that once you've read this book, you will feel deeply and completely understood.

As you will soon learn, you are not wrong or broken; you are only early.

PART 1

THE PROBLEM CHILD ISN'T THE PROBLEM

CHAPTER 1

THE MISUNDERSTANDING

Highly sensitive people are often labeled as "difficult," "dramatic," or "unstable," not because something is wrong with them, but because they perceive things that others cannot.

In families, workplaces, and cultures that fear the truth, this sensitivity can become a threat. As a result, the sensitive individual is blamed, misunderstood, and cast into the role of the scapegoat. The problem child was never the problem.

The problem child is simply the sensitive one who highlights the denied issues within the family system and society. The scapegoat role is not a true identity, but as children, we often do not understand this difference.

Let me share a little of my story.

I grew up in the Midwest during the eighties and nineties. From an early age, I was sensitive to everything around me. My mother recalls how I could absorb the stress of my environment as if there were no separation between my feelings and those of others. She tells stories about how I sensed the marital issues she and my father faced before I was even old enough to comprehend them.

I was not only energetically and emotionally sensitive, but I was also keenly sensitive to textures, colors, lighting, anything you can think of. These sensitivities set me apart from my peers, and they became particularly apparent in school. While I had abilities and talents that were beyond my years, I struggled to take tests and follow written instructions in the conventional way. Honestly, I often found alternative methods that made more sense to me.

I was very active in sports and music, but my favorite thing was my imagination. I had imaginary friends and even psychic abilities; I could predict events based on feelings I sensed. In elementary school, I told my best friend that I felt I was about to get a call that my grandfather had passed. I was sad and started to cry when the nurse walked into our classroom to get me. There was a call for me. Yes, my grandfather had just passed away. We still talk about this story because it was just too clear to deny.

Amid all this, the focus became my differences, which led to frustration for both my teachers and parents. I remember feeling that school was backward and home felt heavy. I struggled with the challenge of not being permitted to find answers in my own way.

I often got math problems right, but they were marked wrong because the process I used was different from what my teachers taught. They suggested I might have a processing problem, especially since my test scores were low. The truth was that my brain simply worked differently.

At that time, being different was often seen as a deficit. Before I knew it, at just seven years old, I was taken to a psychiatrist for an IQ test. My mother, a schoolteacher, had a very linear approach to learning and couldn't understand why I wasn't meeting expectations. I was exceptional in some areas and falling behind in others. For me, the issue was less about my learning abilities and more about my difficulty processing distractions, which were diverting my focus.

I also want to highlight that many sensitive kids are multidimensional thinkers. My home environment was unstable, and I struggled to focus or relax. I dealt with daily anxiety and unexplained fears and had no outlet for my feelings except through sports, friends, or creative pursuits.

The IQ test revealed that I had an almost genius-level IQ at age seven, but my test scores did not reflect that intelligence. Due to this disparity, I was diagnosed with ADHD and prescribed Ritalin. The most impactful part of this experience was being told I was nearly a genius yet would likely never reach my full potential. This made me feel as though there was something inherently wrong with me that I couldn't fix.

That day, my heart sank, and despair set in. I had hoped the doctor would understand my situation. I wished she would say there was nothing wrong with me and help me overcome the shame I felt. I hoped she would recognize that my answer of "None" to the question, "How many feet does a cat have?" was technically accurate because, in a literal sense, cats have paws, not feet.

Unfortunately, I received the message that I was approaching things incorrectly. I thought I was expected to look deeper into the question, which is simply how my mind works.

After spending an hour with her, during which she acknowledged my brightness, I hoped she would call in my family and explain that I needed a supportive environment where I could feel understood; after all, there was nothing wrong with me.

All I ever wanted was for everyone to get along and have some emotional consistency. However, they did not consider any potential underlying emotional issues, nor did they celebrate my differences. They failed to see that I might be neurodivergent, struggling to fit into a neurotypical system.

I am highly sensitive and struggled to fit into an emotionally chaotic home. Unfortunately, my family viewed my symptoms as the sole issue. They failed to recognize the underlying family dysfunction and instead focused on what was "wrong" with me.

The day of the IQ test was the day I became the family's scapegoat. My family was in denial about the immense stress I felt due to their lack of understanding, and as a result, I was labeled with ADHD and held responsible for everything. Whenever there was a problem, it was, "She's overreacting; it must be her ADHD." "She's not focusing; it must be her ADHD," or even, "She's being difficult; that's a symptom of her ADHD." I lost my identity; I was defined solely by my label.

This led to toxic shame. The truth about sensitive or neurodivergent people is that we tend to be truth-tellers and live authentically by nature. Unfortunately, society often does not empower us to be our true selves. Instead, we are judged by how well we adhere to rules and societal conditioning and how perfectly we fit into established norms.

Many highly sensitive, neurodivergent children receive the "ADHD" label simply because they think differently and don't conform to an outdated system. Some scapegoats never receive a label; they are just labeled as being "bad," "wrong," or "not enough," often without any real justification. This is largely due to our reactions to others' inability to understand us.

I understand my ADHD as a heightened focus, not a deficiency. My attention was not lacking; it was selective. While Ritalin helped me concentrate on tasks I found uninteresting, it also disconnected me from my deeper self, which is crucial for sensitive individuals. It created internal stress and identity issues stemming from the stigma associated with my label and the shame surrounding it.

Ritalin numbed my emotions and dulled my mind in a way that hampered my ability to truly tune into myself. It served as a band-aid for my heightened emotions and lack of focus in school, but it was not a cure. The main point is that there is no cure for something that is not a problem, but rather a difference.

Our society does not think holistically or search for root causes. Instead, it often promotes dependency on medications for financial gain through ongoing treatments. Looking back on this time in my life, I was one of the first ADHD kids in my school, and there was little understanding or even interest in how to nurture my differences. Instead, those differences were disempowered.

Many of us original ADHD kids carried the weight of shame associated with the label, which suggested flaws and dysfunction. I empathize with those of you who resonate with the label; I understand our stories vary. If I had been given my diagnosis at an older age and informed about the positive aspects of ADHD, my sense of self would have been entirely different.

I want to share something important: many of you walk around seeking a label for yourselves, while others hate labels altogether.

In the past, there was a societal system that struggled to understand these experiences, and that was incredibly isolating. However, this discussion isn't about labels for the sake of categorization, but rather about refining the original definition.

It's also about the growing number of people entering the world at this time, ready to facilitate systemic change. I believe that ADHD is a genuine condition with challenges, but I also know it is very misunderstood.

According to the National Survey of Children's Health (NSCH), there was a 42 percent increase in children in the United States being diagnosed with ADHD between the years 2003 and 2011. This is one of the steepest accelerations on record in U.S. data. It has been said that this increase was too large to be explained by population growth alone. Other countries did not experience such a large spike.

The increase could be due to diagnostic expansion or to more of us entering the school system and being recognized at that time. We don't know for sure, but based on my personal research and insight, I see this as a time of greater awakening.

In my opinion, this diagnosis is shaped by the type of system we live in. It's like being a dolphin raised in a forest. If we shift our focus from the negative stigma surrounding ADHD and concentrate on its misunderstood positive aspects, we will come to realize that we are not flawed; rather, we are evolved.

Many of you know this, but you seek validation in ways you have not yet seen. The system doesn't get it, and your family may not, either. You are not wrong; you are simply different.

Honestly, after empowering myself, the differences I've discovered in myself are things I wouldn't want to live without.

They are incredible tools that help me break down complex topics and connect with life on a deeper level.

When we recognize that we are all born perfect for our purposes, we can see that the difficulties we face are not assigned by God but stem from an outdated system. Personally, my heightened sensitivity and ADHD allow me to hyper-focus on my interests, uncover deeper truths through insight, and serve my work and purpose as an empathic entrepreneur and teacher.

At the time of my diagnosis, the educational system only recognized one way of learning, one way of testing, and one way to measure intelligence. Emotional intelligence didn't even exist as a well-known concept in the 1980s, and there was a significant lack of emotional support or understanding both at home and in school.

From a young age, I knew that my symptoms reflected my personal refusal to be misunderstood or confined to a box. I should also mention that I learned better when I liked the teacher and felt understood.

Let's not forget that my mother had a master's degree in education and worked as a high school business teacher. We weren't deeply attuned to each other, and we struggled to connect. For many years, I battled to express my feelings and, even more, to understand them. Navigating this journey without anyone who could relate to me on this level was incredibly challenging.

Having a difference like this can make you feel inherently inferior. It becomes an excuse for others to project their hidden shame onto you. It's crucial to recognize that emotionally immature people often blame others as a way to relieve the negative feelings caused by inadequacies that they cannot accept in themselves.

In 2001, I read a book called *The Indigo Children* by Lee Carroll and Jan Tober. It was the first time I had heard this term. The book described children with a different consciousness, often labeled with ADHD. It was the first time I'd read something that sounded so similar to my experience. The term "indigo child" comes from the color of their aura and the essence of their soul. It signifies higher levels of insight, intuition, and multidimensional thinking.

Indigos are often labeled as having ADHD. No matter what the label or explanation is, the fact is that people have been noticing this for quite a while now. I remember thinking all those years ago that maybe many highly sensitive people have been scapegoated by their families and society simply because they have a different consciousness than what is typically understood.

Another trait of indigo children is how they struggle to focus on subjects that don't align with their spiritual missions. This resonated with my own experience, and I continued to search for deeper answers.

As I gained experience working with people, I found that many empathic, highly sensitive individuals I encountered had been emotionally sensitive children who'd never felt understood or empowered. I use the term "spiritually sensitive" to describe a person whose aura and soul essence are characterized by deep insight, intuition, and multidimensional thinking.

You may have noticed that Lee Carroll wrote an endorsement for this book. The story of how we met, some twenty years after I first read his book, is one to tell. Lee's team reached out to me in 2025 to be featured in his Indigo Emergence summit. Of course, I said yes, and it felt like meeting a soul family. Since that appearance, Lee, his partner Monika, and I have collaborated many times.

It felt like a full-circle moment since I knew I was about to finish this book. I told them about it, and they validated that even though I had started writing this over a decade ago, the time to finish it was now. Again, you can't miss what is meant for you. And also, sometimes, it can be annoying to be ahead of the times.

The spiritually sensitive people I have worked with are often diagnosed with ADHD, and I have come to realize that many highly sensitive people are scapegoated for having a consciousness that differs from the norm, creating a massive wound in them.

Spiritually sensitive and emotionally sensitive people struggle to focus on topics that are not related to their interests or spiritual path. It's not that we want to rebel; rather, we are so connected to our internal guidance system that we lack the ability to feel inspired or interested in subjects that aren't aligned with our calling. The issue arises when we can't find our interests in any conventional societal career choice. That may sound strange to some, but when you consider the influence of certain blood types on behavior and food choices, it can lead to a deeper understanding.

For instance, people with O blood type tend to be meat eaters, hunters, and gatherers. Personally, I am blood type O, and as a child, I preferred running around to sitting still. I would rather explore than be taught in a conventional way. I often choose my own path rather than following the crowd.

There is a well-known evolutionary hypothesis often called "hunters versus farmers," originally articulated by Thom Hartmann and later explored by evolutionary psychologists and anthropologists. The core idea is that traits we now label as ADHD were adaptive advantages in hunter-gatherer societies rather than deficits.

Many clients with ADHD can relate to feelings of emotional intensity, being driven or easily distracted, and experiencing periods of hyperfocus or total lack of focus. Additionally, we often encounter rejection sensitivity, which is frequently misunderstood.

Rejection sensitivity feels like you might die at the prospect of being rejected by someone you like or love. As adolescence starts and hormones surge, this can happen out of nowhere. Later, I will discuss the narcissistic relationships that many highly sensitive individuals, scapegoats, and those with ADHD often find themselves in. When someone is scapegoated at home or in school, this pattern can continue into intimate relationships until it is addressed and healed.

There is a much deeper reason for these patterns than mere relational issues; it has to do with the brain chemistry that develops as a result of trauma.

Dr. Gabor Maté is a renowned Hungarian-Canadian physician, author, and speaker known for his influential work on trauma, addiction, ADHD, autoimmune disease, and childhood development. He believes that ADHD is not something children are born with. It develops when a sensitive nervous system grows up in an environment where emotions aren't met or mirrored, such as homes where stress is high, even subtly, or where caretakers are overwhelmed, depressed, distracted, or emotionally absent.

In such environments, the child has to adapt to feel safe or connected. The brain then organizes around hypervigilance, distraction, and emotional regulation struggles. In Maté's words, "Genes may create sensitivity, but the environment shapes whether ADHD emerges" (Gabor Maté, *Scattered Minds: A New Look at the Origins and Healing of Attention Deficit Disorder*, 1999).

I have seen many highly sensitive people who were traumatized, and from there, I have seen many labels emerge. For people who believe the condition is genetic because a parent also had it or maybe had it but was undiagnosed, I say it is generational trauma that was never healed and therefore passed on for the next generation to break the cycle.

When we experience trauma, we can also become trauma-bonded to ourselves, life, and others. The trauma bonds we form often reflect the traumatic experiences we had early in life. When we don't have unconditional love or acceptance, we feel traumatically bonded to our caregivers, friends, and authority figures. When this is our first attachment, we can experience an attachment injury, and therefore, the way our system registers connection can be traumatic. I will go deeper into this topic in Chapter 4, where I address toxic relationships.

Many of the children and young adults I coach say they feel alone or like they only have one or two friends, rather than being part of a larger group. Sensitive kids tend to pick up on the intentions of others, even when those intentions aren't explicitly communicated. This sensitivity can feel overwhelming, especially in a group setting with varying opinions, making one-on-one interactions much more comfortable. I, too, have always had only one or two close friends. In fact, the first friend I made in kindergarten is still my best friend today, forty years later!

It's been said that highly sensitive individuals possess a strong moral compass and are incredibly loyal. They can often sense honesty and may experience physical discomfort when confronted with deception. When they find someone they can truly trust, they tend to be loyal for life.

However, the group dynamics present in school can be filled with unspoken stressors. While I generally got along with everyone, received birthday party invitations, and enjoyed hosting sleepovers, I still experienced sensitivity to rejection, both imagined and real.

Questions often arise, such as, "Did she look at me wrong?" "Does she not like me?" "Did I do something to upset her because she didn't call me back?" This creates confusion because we may be sensitive to someone else's emotions even if they don't confirm what we feel. It is also possible to feel both introverted and extroverted, depending on the situation.

Each person's experience growing up as a sensitive individual is unique, yet a common thread ties us together: we are multidimensional feelers, and that can feel like a lot to handle. While some sensitive people may take on the role of scapegoat, they might not always confront authority like I did. Many scapegoats endure quiet suffering until they can't handle staying quiet and start to navigate the trauma that comes with being awake in a sleepy world.

A common experience for me growing up was always worrying about whether I was liked. I felt so misunderstood at home that I remember walking around with this constant feeling of impending shame. This looked like a hidden closet inside myself that I could hide in if I felt shamed by someone or even perceived that I wasn't being liked or talked about. I was always ready to retreat into my private world of feelings.

Many of my clients also talk about this inner space. There isn't anywhere to go where they feel safe, so they create this inner world of retreat. This can feel very isolating at times, but it is also a place to put the parts of us that are not mirrored in the outside world. Though this creates a rich inner world, it also leaves us feeling disconnected from the people around us.

Many years later, after I had done the majority of my healing, the shame closet I had, where I would put all of my unmet feelings, was what ultimately became my treasure of insight. I would analyze what I was feeling and look for deeper possible reasons for it. I remember thinking this part of myself was my most intimate.

This is often the part of ourselves that gives rise to deep empathy for others. As we learn to understand ourselves, this shame transforms into insight.

Take this quick quiz:

Questionnaire

Are You the Family Scapegoat, a Cycle Breaker, a Highly Sensitive Individual, Neurodivergent—or (Like Me) All of the Above?

Part 1: The Scapegoat

1. Were you blamed for tensions or conflicts that you did not create?

2. Did you feel different in your family without understanding why?

3. Were your emotions treated as the problem rather than as a response to your environment?

4. Did you learn to doubt your perceptions because others dismissed them?

5. Were you labeled as dramatic, too sensitive, or difficult?

6. Did things remain calm when you minimized yourself or shrank your presence?

7. Did you feel responsible for managing the emotional dynamics around you?

8. Did you feel punished for acknowledging what was actually happening?

If you answered "yes" to most of these questions, you may have been the scapegoat who carried what others would not face. However, you can now become the cycle breaker.

Part 2: The Sensitive One

1. Are you overwhelmed by strong colors, sounds, or environments?

2. Do you quickly and intensely feel other people's emotions?

3. Are you deeply affected by injustice, cruelty, or dishonesty?

4. Do you feel misunderstood because your reactions are more intense than those of others?

5. Can you sense subtle shifts in mood, energy, and dynamics?

6. Do you need beauty and meaning in your life to help you regulate your emotions?

7. Do you have an unusually close connection with animals?

If you answered "yes" to most of these questions, you likely have a finely tuned nervous system and may be highly sensitive.

Part 3: Are You Neurodivergent?

1. Did you struggle in school but thrive outside of structured systems?

2. Were tests, memorization, or rigid schedules harder than real-life problems?

3. Do you focus deeply on what interests you and struggle with what doesn't?

4. Were you labeled as "scattered," "lazy," or "underperforming" despite clearly showing intelligence?

5. Do you think in patterns, images, or connections rather than in linear steps?

6. Do you perform best with autonomy rather than supervision?

7. Do traditional productivity systems fail you?

8. Have you been diagnosed with ADHD or suspect that you might fit that description?

If you answered mostly "yes," you may be neurodivergent, possessing a nonlinear mind that is often labeled dysfunctional in a linear system.

Are you a cycle breaker?

1. Do you feel that the cycle of dysfunction needs to end with you?

2. Do you want to do things differently from your parents?

3. Have you felt pressured to remain small to maintain harmony in your life?

4. Do you feel called to create a life that is completely different from the one you grew up in?

5. Do you feel like you outgrow environments faster than others?

6. Do people project their issues onto you?

7. Do you live more consciously than those who came before you?

8. Are you blamed for issues more often than not?

Cycle breakers are frequently punished before they are understood. If you answered "yes" to most of these questions, you were born with a heightened awareness meant to awaken others.

The good news is that there are many like you, so you are not alone. It is important to seek each other out in order to come together and serve the purpose of spreading spiritual truths and replacing outdated views with new ones. You are stepping into your roles as spiritually relevant leaders of the future.

Cycle breakers are born aware, but the question is: why now? The short answer is evolution. You might feel like there is no one to guide you, but I found guidance within. Ultimately, part of the contrast we experience in our families and systems shows us who we aren't, so that we can become clearer about who we are.

Astrological changes are underway. We are transitioning from the Piscean to the Aquarian Age. You are the frontrunners of the Aquarian Age, which is all about oneness, breaking down labels, and living from a more holistic perspective.

As authority shifts, we are awakening as a planet and now look to highly sensitive and empathic people to lead us into a new way of living. Spiritually sensitive people are here to help us live lives of integrity, which means being true to ourselves and honoring courage, trust, and love for ourselves and others in our authentic forms.

Many of us are nonconformists who cannot easily fit into categories or boxes. Many struggle with this journey until we come to understand that there is a higher calling. Connecting with your higher guidance (God, source, whatever you want to call it) is the way.

Our impulsivity is our direct connection to what is true for us.

When we sense that something is out of emotional or spiritual alignment, we feel an urgency to respond. Our sensitivity, both physical and emotional, enhances our awareness of multidimensional energies.

Daydreaming serves as our way of visualizing and connecting to something beyond ourselves, while also helping us cope with the boredom we experience in school or at work. We are not here to be a part of the matrix. We are inventors, creatives, entrepreneurs. We are here to pave our own way.

Many of us are aware of our preferences from a young age. If the subjects we study in school do not align with our higher purpose, we may feel little motivation to engage with them. What we truly desire is a connection to our higher selves; when this connection is undervalued or unacknowledged, we often find ourselves labeled as "uncooperative."

Highly sensitive children have a natural remembrance of spiritual law. We push against what blocks our heart, binds our mind, and numbs our knowing of who we are as divine and right on time.

Chapter Summary

- **The Scapegoat:** Highly sensitive children often become "scapegoats" in dysfunctional families. Because they perceive and react to hidden tensions or truths that others deny, the family labels the child as "the problem" to avoid addressing systemic issues.
- **Neurodivergence is not a Deficit:** ADHD and other labels are often "multidimensional" or "nonlinear" ways of thinking. The struggle isn't a lack of intelligence, but a mismatch between a sensitive nervous system and a rigid, linear educational or societal system.
- **Impact of Trauma and Environment:** According to Dr. Gabor Maté, ADHD symptoms can emerge when

a sensitive child lacks emotional mirroring or lives in a high-stress environment, leading to "attachment injuries" and a brain organized around hypervigilance.

- **The "Spiritually Sensitive" Identity:** The concept of "Indigos," or "spiritually sensitive" individuals, is that people with deep intuition and a strong moral compass struggle to focus on tasks that don't align with their higher purpose or internal guidance system.
- **The Role of the Cycle Breaker:** Those who were once shamed or labeled are framed as "cycle breakers" and "evolved" leaders. Their purpose is to transition society toward a more holistic, authentic way of living (the Aquarian Age), turning their past "shame" into a "treasure of insight."

CHAPTER 2

THE FAMILY ROLE: YOU FRONT-LOADED YOUR KARMA

The highly sensitive one is always the scapegoat, and scapegoating is the mechanism that suppresses emerging consciousness.

Not every family assigns roles, but some do, and whether it is consciously or unconsciously, it is definitely being done unfairly. Inevitably, there will be the child who acts as the stabilizer, the peacemaker, the golden child, and then there's the one who absorbs what no one else is willing to feel.

If you were the child who felt too much, reacted honestly, questioned what didn't make sense, or could not tolerate emotional neglect, you were likely assigned a role you never agreed to: the carrier of denied pain. This chapter is not about blame; it's about context. When pain remains unnamed, it doesn't disappear; it simply moves.

In many families, this pain moves into the most sensitive, intuitive, and truth-oriented child. You were not chosen because you were weak. The sensitive one is not made a scapegoat because they are bad, broken, or deficient. You were chosen because you were the most perceptive in a family that functioned on denial. You reacted to harm. You noticed emotional inconsistency. You felt what others worked hard not to acknowledge. Often, you were also the one trying to keep the peace.

The combination of truth, sensitivity, and empathy can be destabilizing in an emotionally immature system. To survive, the system does what systems do: it places the discomfort onto you. If you're upset, you're the problem. If you're acting out, no one has to look deeper.

This behavior isn't always rooted in conscious cruelty; it's often a form of avoidance, and avoidance requires a container. You didn't create the pain; you contained it. Families, like all systems, have a tolerance level for truth. Anything that exceeds that tolerance must be redirected elsewhere.

This is where you begin your journey as the container for generational trauma. When grief isn't processed, anger isn't acknowledged, fear is denied, and shame is buried, the emotional system unconsciously seeks a vessel. I refer to this vessel as "the host." Sensitive children are often ideal vessels and hosts.

You can sense tension in a room while others seem fine. You react to what remains unsaid. Of course, you learn to feel like you are the issue because you can't wrap your mind around how no one else is bothered by this.

You absorb feelings and emotions that have nowhere to land, and as a result, a narrative forms around you. The painful part is that you may be gaslit out of your own truth, leading you to question and doubt your own perception. Often, the emotionally dominant parent constructs a narrative that places the blame on you, not because it's accurate, but because it allows them to avoid accountability.

Their relief comes from your caring about what they cannot face. Over time, this erodes your self-trust. You are told you're wrong so often that you begin doubting your own perceptions.

This is not insecurity; it's systemic gaslighting. You were gradually broken down through cycles of self-doubt.

Being consistently told that you're wrong makes you think there is something wrong with you. The scapegoat, the one who becomes the diagnosed patient, is often projected onto by those who refuse to take accountability for themselves. Eventually, the family turns against you. As they use you as a scapegoat to escape their own denied trauma, they find temporary relief.

The good news is that the empathic, sensitive person who feels deeply is also the one who has the potential to heal completely.

For many years, you may feel isolated in your reality. The outside world generally has no idea what is occurring within the family dynamic. While the family maintains an exterior that contradicts the interior, they function based on image. For them to feel safe and preserve this image, you must remain labeled as "the problem child."

This is how you learn to earn love, but it never truly works. Many scapegoated children spend years trying to achieve safety. You strive to be better, calmer, more pleasing, more composed, and more successful, yet the better you become at this, the less it seems to work.

It's not because you are failing; it's because you were set up to fail. Your role was never about improvement; it was about containment.

As long as you are seen as the problem, the family can maintain its façade. If you were released from this role, their unaddressed truths would surface. The more you strive for perfection, the more you abandon your true self.

Often, clients will ask me if their parents knew what they were doing. The truth is that many do and many don't. They feel triggered by you because they are so unaware of their own inner worlds.

But think about a trigger for a moment. A trigger is something that upsets us so much that we feel we need to get away from it. Someone who has done a lot of inner work can see that what is triggering them is a mirror of something within themselves that needs healing. A person who is not very self-reflective will see a trigger as something to reject.

In such a system, the choice becomes agonizing: abandon yourself to survive within the family or abandon the family to reclaim yourself. As a child, you don't get to choose, but your body remembers.

As a child, you often have no choice but to accept your circumstances. However, as you grow older, you may find that you are unconsciously treating your inner child the same way you were treated as a child. Eventually, you will come to realize that the coping mechanisms you developed to stay safe within a toxic environment are now causing you harm. As you heal, the coping mechanisms need to be upgraded, or what once made you safe from a toxic system now makes you unsafe in a healthy environment.

I remember the first time I was scapegoated. I was in kindergarten, during playtime, climbing on the jungle gym. I was so engaged that I didn't hear Mrs. Fordyce say time was up. I glanced over at my classmates, who were all watching me, and saw the stern, angry expression on the teacher's face.

She made an example of me in front of the entire class, saying that I didn't listen. It was heartbreaking because I had no idea I had done anything wrong. Later in life, I realized that this incident hurt me so deeply because it mirrored the role I had already been put into at home. If I had grown up in a supportive family, a small issue like that wouldn't have affected me so much.

We often blame ourselves for caring too much or being overly sensitive. It's important to recognize that there's a reason we feel criticism so deeply and painfully. It's not that we are too sensitive; it's due to the programming we've received.

When you're young and dependent on your parents and other adults, gaining their approval can feel essential for your survival. I can still recall the pure terror I felt as a child when I was blamed for things I didn't do. No matter how much I pleaded, my innocence was never believed.

I felt trapped. I could scream and yell, but that often led to timeouts or withheld affection. Alternatively, I could try to distract myself from what was happening and tune out.

Tuning out became my coping mechanism. I would daydream, draw in class, and create fairy tales in my mind to escape my reality. I often imagined a future life that would allow me to break free from my painful situation.

When you have to dissociate from your reality to survive, you get accustomed to distracting yourself from anything that requires focus, and you start to hyper-focus on anything that interests you enough to ease the discomfort. This is not a character flaw; it's an adaptation.

I explain to my clients that they have "front-loaded" their karma. I mean this not as a punishment; it simply relates to timing.

Front-loading karma means you've experienced things early that others have postponed. The contrast between what you experience and what others experience pushes you to seek beyond your conditions. You have carried grief that was never mourned, anger that was never permitted, truths that threatened stability, and pain that had nowhere to go. While others delayed this part of their growth, you were forced to embody it.

When we front-load karma, we experience a stark contrast to who we are early on. This can set the stage for wanting to leave home early, have huge success, and escape. This explains why scapegoated children often feel wiser than their years. They may mature physically and still carry emotional trauma and responsibility without consent. You were processing emotional material that the system couldn't handle at the time. This can make you think you are not capable, but in reality, you are more capable than the family you grew up in.

It's interesting how many scapegoats feel incapable. You were born into a family that provided a stark contrast, which ultimately forced you to awaken to your true self, yet many people get caught in a false identity. You hold on to shame for so long that it can feel impossible to break free of it.

The scapegoat faces a challenging start in life, but there is also a gift in the ability to awaken to a better way. To break these cycles, we need to integrate our sensitivity and begin asking important questions.

At some point, often in adulthood, something shifts. We realize: *I cannot keep carrying what was never mine.* This is when the role of the scapegoat becomes dangerous to the family system, not because we are attacking it, but because we stop absorbing the blame. We start asking ourselves: *What if the pain didn't start with me? What if my reactions make sense?* We begin to see our role as functional rather than defective. This marks the birth of the cycle breaker.

The cycle breaker is the one who returns responsibility, refuses to accept inherent shame, and chooses truth over belonging. This is not rebellion; it is maturation. Letting go of the scapegoat role without rejecting yourself is essential.

Releasing the scapegoat role does not require confrontation, blame, or rejection. It requires reassignment. Internally, you assert, *I release what was never mine to carry.*

You stop explaining yourself to those who are invested in misunderstanding you. You stop doing emotional labor unconsciously and cease identifying with pain that does not belong to you.

You retain your sensitivity, depth, and discernment. What you let go of is false responsibility.

Remember, you did not fall behind in life; instead, you were working to advance emotionally and consciously. You did not fail; you were trying not to fail a system that failed you.

You were advanced enough to try to protect yourself, but you were forced into protecting your family's lies. The work ahead is not about healing what is wrong with you but about reclaiming what has always been right.

I often tell my clients, "There was never anything wrong with you; what's wrong is that you still think there is." What is wrong with you is that you were done wrong and blamed for their behavior.

It's not about healing mistakes; it's about claiming that people are mistaken about what really happened to you. You no longer need to carry everyone else's unfinished business or heal everyone else's unhealed wounds.

You took on the pain so the family lineage could survive. Now it's time to take on the truth so it can evolve. This is not a burden; it is a calling. However, scapegoats often feel alone. Even when siblings are present, there is also triangulation.

The dominant parent must remain in control at all times. This parent will tell each sibling negative stories about the others to gain their loyalty. In healthy families, siblings band together, feeling support, friendship, and kinship, but in a toxic family, the scapegoat is left alone, and the family embraces a false narrative about that child. This can feel incredibly isolating and shame-inducing. It can feel as if you were born into a family you were never a part of.

I often refer to this as the "sensitive orphan." Many of the scapegoats I work with feel that they never had the support they needed. They internalize the belief that they don't deserve it, yet they still strive to belong. When we come to understand that we didn't belong not because of ourselves, but because of the wounded system we were born into, we can start to awaken to a better identity.

It wasn't until I was in my thirties that I realized it might not have been me. I had done so much work on myself, like many of you, yet I continued to repeat certain patterns. Those patterns didn't break until I upgraded my identity and realized there was nothing wrong with me; the system I was born into was very, very flawed.

When I was able to observe my situation more neutrally, instead of feeling burdened by the unhealed emotions, I noticed that many family members coped with past wounds by avoiding or numbing them. Meanwhile, I was living a really good life that I was genuinely proud of.

When this dawned on me, I asked myself why I was still carrying around this scapegoat wound. Like many scapegoats, I had internalized the past negativity and tried to achieve my way out of it.

However, once I reached a certain point, I recognized that someone capable of successful relationships in life cannot be that broken. Someone who once carried such heavy emotional pain for others cannot be entirely incapable. Even someone who followed all of her dreams and fought for herself despite the pain beneath the surface cannot be truly embarrassed.

As you start to re-examine your role, you will see that it wasn't about you. Your role was to cover up the stories of everyone else. The family dynamic changes when you choose to no longer agree with the role they assigned to you. This doesn't mean they suddenly treat you differently; it means that you no longer agree with their treatment, and this is where big change happens.

For many years, I allowed others to talk about me behind my back, spinning narratives that were far from reality and turning family members against me. I quietly continued to live my life as I saw fit. I didn't go completely without contact, but I chose to maintain low contact for about fifteen years.

My niece and nephew, who once idolized me, became distant. They were young kids, so I knew it wasn't their choice. However, I accepted that it was just part of the narrative. And still, I never lived my life in a way that would validate their assumptions.

By this time, I was living vibrantly and confidently because I believed that the truth would eventually come out. Many scapegoats are afraid to let themselves enjoy their lives because being who they truly are is what led to their abandonment in the first place. However, I already felt abandoned, and I had married into a new family. At one point, I remember thinking I had outrun the pain of the past.

I took time to discover my true self and pursue my new dreams. I worked on ending the pattern of overachieving. Instead of being dependent on maintaining a perfect life to prove my worth, I began to relax my need for perfection and started embracing authenticity. One Christmas marked a turning point for me.

In 2018, I lived in a gorgeous house in Malibu, California. I drove a Maserati and was married. I thought I had checked the boxes at that point in my life. I had four stepchildren and was deeply involved in building my business. That Christmas, I invited my mom and stepdad, who lived in Florida, to join us in Malibu. I was hoping to show them how great my life had become. I thought this might help them see me for who I truly am. After all the work I'd put in, I was still trying to impress them for some reason.

It's interesting how healing works; I had done so much work on my inner world but had left out the piece that mattered most. When we are truly embodied, we no longer need to show it; we just are it. If you are still trying to show, prove, or convince, you are not yet convinced yourself. This disconnection can be painful, but it can also lead to breakthroughs. This was about to be the breakthrough I needed most and had also always tried to avoid.

That Christmas turned out to be an extraordinary turning point in my life. I thought I would prove to them that I was worthy of them. Instead, what went down that Christmas became my proof that I had already embodied my self-worth enough to no longer need their approval.

We had lobster that Christmas in Malibu, and we decided to drive to Vegas to show my mother and stepfather an even better time. I was sure to buy them amazing gifts and not leave anything out.

But then it happened! I faced the moment I thought I had escaped. I thought I had set everything up perfectly to avoid the inevitable. Upon returning from Vegas to my Malibu home, I noticed someone had gone into my office, which I had locked while I was away. My stepkids had full access to the house, so I just assumed it was one of them. I said, "Someone broke into my office. This is not making me happy."

As I went back downstairs, I could see everyone upstairs through the glass staircase and hear what they were saying. On my way back up, I caught a glimpse of my mother and heard her say, "You should put her back on Ritalin. There is something wrong with her."

For context: I had not taken any medication since I was seventeen, about twenty years earlier.

At that instant, I knew the cycle was about to break. I'd spent years learning, doing shadow work, and building a life I was proud of. The scapegoat role no longer fit.

I walked up the stairs. Everyone looked stunned. They couldn't believe what they had just heard, and neither could I.

I confronted her directly: "What the hell did you just say?"

She denied it: "I didn't say anything, honey. What do you think you heard?"

I asked the room: "Did all of you hear that?"

They were all stunned into silence, just looking at me and then looking down.

"Okay," I said, "that's the last time you'll ever do that to me again."

I stormed into my bedroom with the big double doors and slammed them shut. Everyone was left in shock, and slowly, they dispersed. This time, instead of ganging up on me, no one said a word.

My stepson muttered, "Wow, your mom's really something."

My husband, shaped by his own family dynamics, asked, "What are you doing?"

"What do you mean, what am I doing?" I replied.

"That behavior is toxic."

He seemed unsure and preoccupied with his own discomfort, so he couldn't comfort me—but I was fine. Something shifted inside me; I was done. I barely slept that night, yet I got up around 5 a.m. for a spin class with a friend. I felt the trauma in my body, but I stayed true to myself and didn't speak to them for the rest of the day.

After spin class, I went right into self-care. I booked myself a session with my therapist, followed by a massage, and ended with a manicure. I had learned my way of self-soothing, and I was applying it heavily. I was nurturing my inner child in the face of being attacked. After what I had just gone through, not to mention endured my entire life, I deserved some pampering.

I needed to get grounded and cared for so I could take the next bigger step. I promised myself that I would do whatever it took to never let this happen again. That was the day my role changed for good.

When I returned home, they told a sob story about there being no food. I calmly replied, "There's food in the fridge." I stayed composed; I did not collapse or play the part they

wanted me to.

Eventually, I texted my mom: *"I feel it's best that you go home today. I'll arrange a ride to the airport. I can't allow this to continue. I won't be placed in a role that isn't mine. I am no longer your diagnosed patient."*

She burst into my room, clearly upset, and spoke angrily. After saying things I won't repeat, she left in tears, telling me I had been cruel.

The good news was that my husband had heard everything. He walked in and said, "That's not what I heard"—the first time others recognized the reality I'd been living.

My mother left that day, and I didn't speak to her for months. It seemed possible we might never reconcile.

Even as I stood my ground, panic and anxiety rose up to be released. My body shook as years of unresolved trauma came out. I'd seen multiple doctors trying to explain my breathing difficulties and the numbness in my left hand. When I researched the spiritual meaning of the left side of the body—often associated with the past—it felt like confirmation that this was tied to long-buried wounds.

Months later, my mom reached out to me over something trivial. I told her directly, "Don't contact me unless you're ready to acknowledge what happened." I was no longer afraid of the narrative; my only objective was either accountability or no contact.

To my surprise, Mom shared that she had been experiencing panic attacks. She said she felt like her arm had been cut off by being distant from me. She was dealing with anxiety, just as I was. She had almost identical symptoms, but on the opposite side of her body. This was beyond interesting to me, but perhaps I had triggered her own release of stored trauma, too.

I often say that once we decide to heal and claim our truth, we can literally see the family lineage shift, too. My experience of this was happening in real time.

I also saw it as the end of absorbing other people's unhealed pain. Once I stopped taking it on, she began to feel it instead. When one person heals, family members can either heal with them or stay in denial—she chose to heal.

She asked if we could take a trip together. I said I would consider it—but only if we used the time to address not just the recent incident but the patterns that had played out for years. I wanted it to be a chance to deepen our mutual understanding.

She vowed, "I'll do whatever it takes to get my daughter back." That shocked me to my core. I'd spent so long earning her approval that the offer to reconnect caught me off guard, but I agreed to go.

Over seven days, I asked the questions I'd long wanted answered: Why had I never truly known my sister? Why had she discouraged my stepdad from getting close? Why had I been labeled the family problem so early on?

She answered as honestly as she could. "Candace, we didn't understand your gifts back then. If there had been a program for gifted kids, you would have been in it. Instead, they medicated you. "We simply didn't know better."

She acknowledged that my sensitivity allowed me to perceive dynamics between her and my father that they hadn't recognized. She admitted she's been stuck seeing me as the problem child and hadn't really known me as an adult.

When I asked why she couldn't let me outgrow that role, she could only say, "I don't know." I offered, "Perhaps you needed me to be the excuse for how you treated me. I forgive you, and I hope you can forgive yourself."

By the end of the trip, she said, "You're right—I've never allowed myself to see you outside that identity. I didn't question it until now. You made it difficult at times. I've watched you grow, and you're doing remarkable things. You've made yourself important in the world.

She told me that she saw me taking my difficulties and using them to help others heal. When I asked her why those difficulties existed, she said she thought it was because I was just different and maybe ahead of my time.

Since then, my mother and I have had repairs. It is obvious that she no longer puts me in the old role. It's almost like she had a permission slip to release me from the role now that I had done the same. Today, my mother and I have a very different relationship. There is respect, and we share many similarities. We enjoy many of the same things, and it has been very healing to relate to her from a place of love rather than stress or disconnection.

Not everyone gets to repair in this lifetime, but I want you to know that it's possible, even if your parents have passed or you are not able to get healing with them. The biggest healing happens when you release yourself from the role. If they can mirror that with you, it's amazing, but if they can't, it is important that you continue to honor your journey and live as your free self.

I feel lucky that I got to heal this. While things are not perfect, they are now, at least, in their correct place.

Chapter Summary

- **The Scapegoat as the Family Container:** In dysfunctional families, the most sensitive and truth-oriented child is often assigned the role of scapegoat. This child becomes the unconscious container for denied grief, shame, anger, and generational trauma so the family system can avoid facing its deeper wounds.
- **Systemic Gaslighting and False Identity:** Repeated blame, invalidation, and projection cause the scapegoated child to distrust their own perceptions and internalize the belief that something is wrong with them. The chapter reframes this not as a personal deficiency but

as systemic gaslighting within an emotionally immature family structure.

- **"Front-Loaded Karma" and Early Emotional Burden:** The author describes scapegoated children as having "front-loaded" their karma, meaning they are forced to process difficult emotional material early in life that others postpone or deny. This early burden creates wisdom, maturity, and depth but can also produce shame, dissociation, and a desperate drive to escape or overachieve.
- **The Birth of the Cycle Breaker:** Healing begins when the scapegoat realizes the pain did not start with them and stops carrying responsibility for what was never theirs. The cycle breaker emerges by releasing false responsibility, reclaiming self-trust, and choosing truth over the need to belong within a distorted family narrative.
- **Releasing the Role Without Losing the Self:** The chapter emphasizes that freedom does not require blame or dramatic confrontation but an internal reassignment of identity. The sensitive person keeps their empathy, discernment, and depth while letting go of shame, overexplanation, and the compulsion to absorb everyone else's unfinished pain.
- **Repair, Boundaries, and Reclaiming Truth:** Through a later confrontation with her mother, the author shows how breaking the scapegoat role can shift the entire family dynamic. Even though not every family achieves repair, true healing comes when the scapegoated person no longer agrees with the false role and begins living from authenticity rather than inherited shame.

CHAPTER 3

MY AWAKENING AND EXISTENTIAL CRISIS

"The sensitive child suffers most, not from pain, but from the absence of a mirror that can reflect their truth."

— Alice Miller, *The Drama of the Gifted Child: The Search for the True Self*

In the summer before my junior year of high school, something occurred that changed the trajectory of my life. On my sixteenth birthday, I had an out-of-body experience that I often refer to as my spiritual awakening.

But let's back up a little. During my adolescence, I carried a sense of shame and struggled to fit into a system I believed I could not change. As the family scapegoat, much of my positive identity was shaped by my appearance and achievements.

I remember being the smallest kid in every class up until junior year. This made me stand out, allowing clothes to look really good on me and giving me the freedom to excel in sports and feel comfortable in my body.

The Ritalin stunted my growth, or at least delayed it. I wouldn't take it during the summer so my physical growth could catch up. I remember feeling so free in the summertime. This was when I could really just relax and dream. It was a relief not to have to secretly run to the nurse's office every day at lunchtime for the tiny little yellow pill. Since school wasn't my favorite experience, I often dreamed of living an extraordinary life beyond the Midwest town where I grew up.

Junior year is when many kids start planning for college, but I struggled to find a major that resonated with me. I wanted something holistic. I had always been a sensitive, spiritual child, and I knew the mainstream options wouldn't satisfy me. However, I found it challenging to discover a field that matched my interests.

Before the school year began, I took a trip with my church youth group. We were traveling from Chicago, Illinois, to Atlanta, Georgia, for a large youth convention. I had heard stories about how this event changed kids' lives, so I was eager to attend.

Upon arriving in Atlanta, all two thousand of us from different states were ushered into a huge auditorium. I felt completely in my element. I could sense the energy and excitement, but there was also a deep sense of grounding. A preacher was on stage discussing God, our true essence, and who we are as spiritual beings.

During the sermon, something remarkable happened: my consciousness seemed to lift out of my body. I felt as if I were flying around the room, seeing faces I had never encountered before. I could view everything from multiple angles, even seeing myself on the big screen. All of a sudden, I was the preacher, and I even felt like I was with God.

I'm not going to lie, I was starting to think maybe I had died because this experience was otherworldly.

At that moment, I looked around the auditorium and realized that everyone I looked at reflected my own face. It came with an understanding that we are all the same; there is no separation in spirit.

To this day, it sounds odd to talk about because I didn't intend for it to happen, and I couldn't comprehend exactly what occurred. I don't know how long the experience lasted, but at one point, I remember turning to the girl next to me and asking, "Does my face look like yours? Because your face looks like mine." She told me no and asked if I was okay, shaking me back into reality. After that, I felt like I dropped back down, like I returned to my consciousness, but the experience stayed with me.

My life changed that day, and it has never been the same since. It was less about my needing to explain to people and more about the instant effect it had on me. I wasn't asking too many questions because I felt so high, happy, and clear.

I believe I saw my true nature and understood what I was meant to do in this life. The first accurate mirror of who I truly was. The message was that we are all the same: *He is me. She is me. I am them.* There is no separation in truth. It became clear to me that God created us all perfectly for our purposes, and perhaps my purpose would be found outside the societal structure people created, not God. I felt the magnitude of what God meant. I continued to feel the elevation of my mood and my energy. It was truly unreal. I instantly put God on the pedestal where He/She/It belonged.

This was the beginning of my understanding that society might label me, but God never does. People might minimize me, but God never does. This was when I started to explore the idea that society is built on people who have free will. People have the will to create a world of peace and love or of separation. The world is a reflection of people who align with the higher will and also those who use their free will to align with their ego.

This is when I started separating my idea of God from society. I remember feeling helpless in the face of the system, yet empowered by my understanding of it. Keep in mind, I was only sixteen, so this was all completely new to me, but it felt like a profound realization.

This feeling of oneness continued throughout the trip. I felt no separation between myself, others, or God. My attention was drawn to a higher dimension.

On the last night of our trip, the youth group had a birthday party for me and dedicated the song "Staying Alive" to me. Honestly, everything felt perfect at that moment. I had never felt like I belonged so much in my life.

I was so excited and surprised that my group remembered my birthday, let alone celebrated it so specially. I felt more alive than ever before. I experienced a deep understanding, a sense of peace with myself, and an intrigue that felt like the start of a purpose-driven life.

I even remember having a conversation on the bus ride home with a boy I had never gotten along with, and we reached a truce. I was working through this new understanding that I wasn't wrong, and he wasn't wrong; we just needed to communicate. This was another turning point for me in feeling safe among my peers. For the first time, I felt like maybe a lot of my fear of others had to do with my incorrect identity.

When I got home, my family noticed something and asked me why I was acting so differently, seeming free and unaffected by things that would normally bother me. I told them that I finally understood I wasn't bad. I wasn't the problem, and I had a purpose here.

I didn't share the depth of my experience with my parents because I thought they would think I was crazy. I'd always felt invalidated when sharing spiritual concepts or ideas, so I'd learned to keep those thoughts to myself, almost like hiding them away.

As I reflected on this experience, it felt as if the dreams I had for my life were becoming effortless. I noticed this feeling of flow that brought things to me instantly. I remember thinking that this is what alignment felt like and how synchronicities work. I was very clear that I was about to take the road less traveled.

Not long after I got home from this experience, I started having some pretty immediate synchronicities. What felt like alignment was manifestation. One day, I was driving in the car with one of my best friends. We were listening to the radio and heard about an event that evening, a model search. I had just been telling her how I thought I wanted to really go after the dream of becoming a model. I had grown much taller that summer, and I felt the desire to give it a try. We heard that the model search was that night, right across the street from where we were. She looked at me and said, "Candy, it's a sign; we are going." I had nothing prepared. No photos, no experience. I was wearing cutoff jean shorts and Birkenstocks. There was no way I felt ready to walk into a model search. So, we looked at each other and said… "We are doing this!"

Megan and I walked into the Hyatt Hotel and sat in a big room with tons of other potential models. We went up to a big table and "interviewed" with seven top agents from the biggest agencies in New York City. After the interview, we all went and sat down in our seats and waited to be called. They were going to call our names if we made it to the next round, which meant flying to NYC to do a competition. You can imagine the jolt when I heard my name called first. I remember having chills and knowing: this was my path.

But before the big competition in NYC, I had to go back to school. I wasn't sure how to feel for those months as I waited to go to NYC. But in the meantime, I ended up signing with a local agency in Chicago called "Ford Models." Going into my junior year felt amazing. I was armored with a new identity. Not to mention, I had a huge growth spurt that summer, got my braces off, had a spiritual awakening, and became a model. I had a major upgrade. But what I know now about spiritual growth is that once we have a quantum leap, the unhealed wounds will come up stronger to be cleared. At that age, I had no idea what was about to happen.

In the meantime, I felt good and made peace with myself as I found my own success with friends who helped me overlook my old perceived flaws. I was also starting my modeling career. I was finding a lot of positive mirroring, but I also taught myself a backward law of attraction. I started to see that when I felt good, positive things would happen, and when I felt negative, things wouldn't go so well.

The problems started when I was feeling good, but things weren't going my way. I was seeing everything as a response to my feelings, and that's dangerous. This was when I started taking on too much responsibility for other people's treatment of me and for life events, a typical scapegoat struggle.

Now I see this as my way to find a sense of control in a chaotic environment. But this is also how we mistakenly look for God in circumstances. Growing up in an emotionally immature home led me to think that the way I was treated was entirely a reflection of my worth. This was the incorrect idea that would follow me for years.

I began spending more and more time delving into my spiritual beliefs and practices. I was trying to figure out how life worked and how to ensure a positive mirror. I kept bumping up against the reality that sometimes things are just out of our control. This is a tough realization when you don't yet have trust in how life works.

What I was about to learn was: "How we relate to the issue is the issue." My unhealed wounds were dictating my perception of events. But before I really anchored that truth, I was trying to figure out why I was getting so triggered by life.

The Collapse

High school brought this lesson front and center: girls were catty, boys were hormonal, and cliques were the norm. My junior year began as a dream come true. Many clients of mine often report experiencing an identity crisis during this phase, and I am going to explain what I went through in detail.

It all started when the star quarterback of the football team asked me to the homecoming dance. I felt elated. However, that same afternoon, I was shunned by the "cool girl" table I had sat at every day during lunch. I couldn't understand why they were rejecting me, and in that instant, I experienced a life-changing moment. You would think that with the summer I had, I would be confident. But remember, I hadn't made it to the big competition in NYC yet, and I wasn't sure if this modeling thing would pan out. So I was in a very vulnerable spot.

The amount of pain in my solar plexus was unreal. I immediately started to collapse. It was one part rejection sensitivity and another part stored trauma. It is common for spiritually awake kids and teens to have spiritual insight but also still have unhealed sensitivity wounds. This is when we can find ourselves in an identity collapse.

Later, I realized that this was my emotional pain-body being triggered. At the moment of trigger, the intensity of the sensation pulled me into a very vivid vision that felt like a distant memory. It was a vision of me as a baby, seeing myself breastfeeding and there being no milk. This sounds so strange, but it is what came forward as I was going through what felt like a collapse. This experience brought about a deep sense of shame, creating a heavy feeling in my solar plexus, as if someone had gut-punched me and I couldn't move.

I found myself confronted with debilitating shame and uncertainty. I didn't know if God was testing me or what was happening, but it felt like an existential crisis. I faced a pivotal question: should I cling to the old identity or step into the new reality unfolding before me?

I struggled that day at school. I can remember wanting to just go up to the girls at that table and ask them what was going on. Something in me stopped me from doing that. I was afraid of what they might say, but at the same time, I needed answers.

Needless to say, I continued with my day, just feeling perplexed and abandoned.

I went home from school that day and told my mother about the situation. I mentioned the vision I had about her losing her breast milk and how I could not make sense of it, but wanted to share it because it was so real.

My mother stared at me, totally perplexed. She asked me how on earth I could remember that, and I said, "Remember what?" She proceeded to tell me the story of how, when I was eighteen months old and still breastfeeding, she had thought that my father was having an affair and lost her breast milk overnight.

The next morning, when I went to breastfeed, I looked at her with despair. Nothing came through. From that day on, I was a different baby. I had always been a perfect angel, never crying or fussing until that day. From then on, she said, I seemed worried and anxious.

I now see this as my first attachment injury. As a baby, I must have internalized this shocking change in our nurturing style as abandonment, a wound I would carry into adulthood.

Deep shame is one of the biggest unspoken issues faced by highly sensitive teens who feel a disruption in their connections at home. They tend to be hard on themselves, have a strong inner critic, often engage in self-blame, and fall into a pattern of spiritual perfectionism. They may glimpse their true selves but struggle to hold on to that image, blaming themselves for not being strong enough or lacking belief in their abilities.

Now, decades later, I understand that this struggle for identity often first occurs in childhood, but then again in adolescence as we seek autonomy. This phase involves developing a more independent sense of self while still relying on our peers for validation. Think about how intimidating and vulnerable that can be. It is during this time that many teens may fall into eating disorders and substance abuse or seek validation through relationships.

What happens when we lack the mirror we need to maintain our confidence and sense of self? We begin to drown out painful emotions to survive our circumstances. The teen years can be incredibly challenging, and they are particularly incomprehensible for those of us who are energetically and emotionally attuned but lack deep support or an anchored mirror at home.

When I say "other equals mother," I'm referring to how we form relationships that mirror our first experiences with attachment. Going back to my high school story, I was trying to cling to the newfound life I was starting to live. But these friendships felt very uncertain and insecurely attached.

I started to lose my grip. Old patterns of shame resurfaced, and I found myself questioning why this was affecting me so deeply. Was it true? Was God trying to tell me I didn't deserve my dreams? Or was it merely a reflection of my own worries?

Was I doubting myself, and was this turmoil a confirmation that I should have doubt? At that time, I was confused about spiritual concepts and reality.

Did I really not deserve the good things that were starting to come into my life? Was it all just a cruel joke? Or was this all a matter of how I was relating to this issue? Was this a reflection of the inner doubt I still carried, or was this not personal at all? How was I supposed to feel sure of myself if my environment reflected the part of me that was still unsure?

There was no external confirmation, and I didn't understand how to navigate this. This was the start of a much deeper dive into spiritual law. Was life a reflection of worth or a reflection of what we believe about our worth? And if we struggle with worth, how are we supposed to heal that?

Jealousy never crossed my mind. Growing up believing something was wrong with you makes it hard to accept that you might ever be the subject of jealousy. But in fact, jealousy plays a huge role in why we are scapegoated in the first place.

Many scapegoated children grow up with jealous siblings and parents. This might sound unbelievable, but it is a reality. The jealousy, the triangulation between siblings, and family secrets all contribute to the isolation one can feel. I will go into this in detail in Chapter 3.

Before long, the emotional collapse settled into my life.

I did end up going to homecoming with that guy, but we went as friends. I started to shut down emotionally and feared intimacy. My confidence dwindled, leading me to quit playing the violin and piano, activities I had enjoyed for ten years. I dropped gymnastics, which I had practiced since I was three, and also quit my soccer team.

It felt like I was retreating into the shadows of my old identity, full of uncertainty and unable to feel the connection I had previously described. I was losing my anchor, and a massive wave of self-doubt overwhelmed me. I had no tools to help myself out of it and no adult in my life who could comprehend what was happening.

Somewhere in between all of this, I made it to NYC during spring break for the modeling competition. My mother came with me, and although it was very exciting, I was also plagued with self-doubt. I remember us having a great time, and I met new friends. And somehow, at the competition, I was chosen by six of the top modeling agencies in New York. I could not believe I made it. Again, I was not feeling like myself, but I was still able to perform. And this was how I ended up doing life for quite some time. Performing but never resolving the pain beneath.

When I got back from New York, I tried talking to my old therapist, whom we had seen as a family during my parents' divorce, but she couldn't help, either. My friends tried to convince me this really wasn't a big deal, bless their hearts. I remember trying to reach out to my dad's ex-girlfriend, the healer who had been the first person to validate my gifts, but she was nowhere to be found.

No one seemed to understand the existential crisis I was experiencing, and I couldn't fathom why God would put me in a situation with no support. After many months of trying to figure myself out, I decided to approach things differently and adopted a new coping mechanism—perfectionism.

I became so worried about being perfect that I thought I could avoid feeling the pain of rejection. If I were perfect, I reasoned, I wouldn't be rejected and therefore wouldn't have to endure that deep emotional pain. This mindset served as a way to convince myself that there was nothing wrong with me, even though I deeply felt there was. Ultimately, though, I was abandoning myself in the process.

The pain I was trying to prevent wasn't the pain itself; it was the meaning I attached to that pain, the belief that there was something wrong with me. I was now living in a simulation of trying to delay any proof that my fear could be real.

At the same time, I was bypassing my emotions and living as if everything was fine. I decided that if my life looked perfect, then people would no longer see me as flawed. And if I weren't flawed, then I wouldn't be rejected. Little did I know, I was now abandoning my emotional truth.

The summer before my senior year, I headed back to New York for agency meetings and test shoots. I was excited about this career, but I was angry with myself for not being fully present or really enjoying it. I kept thinking that if I could just feel worthy again, everything would improve. Now I was blaming anything that fell short on my emotional state. Once I started my senior year, I decided to join the Pom Squad. I became popular again, attended all the parties, and had a great time. I made the conscious decision to just have fun and to do things I wouldn't normally do. But here is where I began to wonder: *Was this the authentic me, or a mask I'd put on to belong?*

Had I started to turn my real self into an ideal version just to feel accepted and survive socially? Or was I simply learning a new way of being, and my feelings hadn't caught up? Nothing held me back, but I wasn't sure whether this was false confidence or real.

Regardless, it was a memorable year, and I felt like I was getting back on track for a time. However, years later, I would realize that those unhealed deep childhood wounds would resurface.

We cannot run away from childhood wounds. Our inner child must be prioritized above all else. Many people navigate life like I did with a wounded inner child because they lack the tools to heal in the moment. True inner-child work is not fully understood in the world of traditional psychology, either. The help I needed had not yet arrived.

We often bypass the necessary work of true healing. We experience life but don't feel totally emotionally attached to it, as if we are moving through life but not fully in it. A sense of detachment lingers when it comes to ourselves and what we do.

Going back in and doing the inner work has become my specialty. I didn't find anyone to help me, but I relied on my insights to dig deeper and figure it out for myself. Clients who lived with years of frustration and regret have turned their lives around by recognizing this missing piece of their inner child through integration work.

We cannot escape our childhood wounds. Our inner child must come first. We need to choose ourselves to feel chosen. We often do a ton of inner work but bypass the most important part. The integration of the inner child is the only way I have found to teach deep self-partnering. It is the only way we can live a divinely guided life.

Engaging in this healing process has become my forte. In the last couple of years, I have developed the ability in my client sessions to channel their inner child at the ages it hasn't fully integrated yet. I did this for myself for many years without even realizing what I was doing. Now I do it with my clients to help facilitate that final chapter. The way I can explain this process is that when I start talking to a new client, I will get an energetic hit in my body, and within seconds, a number will pop up. An example is "age seven." I will ask the client what happened at seven. As we talk, I will get impressions.

In one session early on, I immediately saw a client as a five-year-old, and she was holding a pink bunny. I asked this new client about the pink bunny when she was five. She burst into tears and told me the story of that pink bunny helping her through a death in the family. She said the bunny was her best friend, and age five was the first trauma. From this original wound, we could make sense of the rest of the story. When we can pinpoint the first time or an early time of pain that was never fully resolved, we can integrate the experience. As we integrate these ages and experiences, the person becomes more integrated and whole. They start to feel more of themselves and more present. Memories can start to surface with this sense of new safety. They come online and can become more open to what is meant for them.

If I hadn't gone through the experiences I'm sharing in this book, I wouldn't have gained the wisdom needed to help others navigate their own journeys. Everything I went through was part of my purpose. And everything you are going through will be part of yours.

If I hadn't had my awakening at sixteen, I may not have opened up to my ability to visualize my own traumas and hold that perspective as I navigated my own emotional healing. If I had had the perfect therapist at the time, then I might not have gone inward so far as to unlock my own insight to one day be able to do this work and guide others. Personal experience is the wisdom we get to share to relate deeply with others.

Healing my relationship with God involved realizing that I wasn't messing things up; God wasn't absent. Instead, it was about walking through the experiences firsthand to gain the wisdom that would ultimately become my calling.

The fact that no one was there to help me back then, and that I had to become that help for myself, solidified my path even further. The occupational hazard we have is being born ahead of our time. However, it's crucial to understand the most significant aspect of being highly sensitive or feeling a lack of validation from home or school: we endlessly search for something, someone, or an achievement to confirm our worth. In reality, our anchored worth comes from self-validation through emotional honesty.

What we truly need is to consistently connect with our inner child and help them feel worthy simply by acknowledging that they exist within us. As we connect to our inner child and start to listen to the messages we receive, we must take action. Our inner child naturally starts to trust us and feel important to us as we live in alignment with our needs and desires. Our nervous systems constantly seek permission to feel safe enough to embrace our true selves.

I glimpsed what it felt like to live in alignment with my true self. Then, when the external world stopped validating that, whether through perceived rejection, past experiences, or challenging times, I lost that alignment. This illustrates how we can become codependent on external realities for our sense of self-worth. It's not our fault. We simply didn't receive the proper validation we needed to develop a solid and healthy sense of who we are. We were misunderstood.

I had many experiences of having moments or glimpses of my alignment throughout the years. I went in and out of it but did not anchor for over a decade. My journey to solidify the reconnection with myself lasted about fifteen years. I now see this time as essential training for my career. I had to go through these experiences and learn to heal myself so that I could genuinely relate to the people I would serve.

I also studied many different modes of healing and spirituality. I dived into Buddhism, Kabbalah… You name it, I studied it. I discovered that no matter what I studied, I always felt aligned when connected to a higher power.

My road to awakening started with my desire to please the modeling industry. I realized that I had chosen a career that mirrored my family dynamic: never perfect enough, even when I excelled. I always felt there was something wrong and constantly felt the need to measure up to some ideal, preventing me from feeling good just as I am. When the emotions are never truly validated or understood by those around us, we live with a constant separation from the deepest part of ourselves.

Ego Career versus Soul Calling

The "ego career" is the path we take to earn validation. The "soul calling" is the path we turn to when we have self-validated.

It's important to realize that this dynamic reflects the family structure. How we do one thing is often how we do all things.

I was already feeling disconnected, and that disconnection stemmed from my attempts to bypass painful wounds without having the tools or guidance to address them. In my journey, I realized that the mental health industry often lacks depth. Therapy didn't seem to help, nor did spiritual practices. Nothing seemed to work. I was left to just move through life half in and half out.

As a result, I spent many years feeling only partially engaged with life, half enjoying myself, seeking validation, and feeling somewhat alive. The other half of me was playing the game of being an image. I was truly caught between being all-in and all-out.

In later chapters, I will talk about the types of relationship patterns that this creates and why. For now, let's dive back into the perfectionism-based industry I found myself working in for two decades.

Entering an industry that thrives on the pursuit of perfection really affected me. Coming from a childhood in which I never felt my true self was enough, I carried that same mindset into my career.

When I was seventeen, I received my first international modeling contract in Japan; they wanted me exactly as I was. However, I remember hearing a small comment: "Can she tone up?" At that time, I was an athlete and hadn't yet started my gymnastics season. I always knew that when the season began, I would tone up naturally, but I was scared of potential rejection. So, in the two months leading up to my departure for Japan, I made sure I was doing everything "right."

I researched every supermodel I could find to learn about their measurements, routines, and lifestyles. I turned myself into a label, a model, rather than remaining true to myself. I began working out differently and closely monitored what I ate, striving to be perfect for the role rather than perfect for me.

During that time, I also changed my Ritalin prescription to a once-daily time-release formula, instead of smaller doses throughout the day. I did this so I wouldn't have to remember to take it while I was away. Once a day sounded better to manage.

What I didn't realize was that time-release Ritalin would suppress my appetite. In the two months before leaving for Japan, my 5-foot, 8 1/2 inch frame, naturally thin at 105 pounds, plummeted to 95 pounds. I lost twenty pounds in just two months, and I looked terrible.

When I arrived in Japan, the agency saw me and immediately rescinded my contract, sending me home with the message that they wanted me just as I was naturally. That was the first time I received the message that I was already enough. Looking back, that realization was a game-changer. They didn't want me to be more perfect or different; I just needed to learn how to trust in myself.

Just to clarify, I eventually returned to Japan five more times and secured the contract each time. I felt the need to prove to myself that I wouldn't mess up what was meant for me. However, that pattern continued for a while. I was now fighting my mind, which was always trying to tell me to be better: once the pressure takes hold, it can consume you. I remember always redoing experiences until I got it totally right.

My goal became about regaining weight, rather than healing the deeper issues related to my weight. The year that I came back from my first trip to Japan, I also went off to college in Connecticut. My mother called the school to make sure they knew about my weight struggles. She was frightened for my life. The protocol I was told the University decided on was that they would weigh me every week to make sure I gained 1.5 lbs a week. If I did, I could stay in school.

This was horrifying. Once again, I found myself going to the school nurse's office, but this time it wasn't for Ritalin; now it was to get weighed. Needless to say, I took myself off Ritalin due to the side effects I was having, but also, I just didn't feel I needed it. The good news is that I never got back on it ever again. Maybe it was because I was away from home. Maybe it was because I found my own way of doing things that worked for me. But I never touched medication again after that, and I got straight A's in college.

After spending several years in the fashion industry, working and living in Japan, Germany, New Zealand, Greece, and Australia. I began to feel that it wasn't fulfilling me, and I no longer felt emotionally sound. The fashion industry's high standards were killing me, and always needing to fit a specific weight, size, height, and measurement criteria felt shallow. I was ready to leave the old safety of standards and move into a new safety with myself.

Even though the beauty ideals and standards varied across all cultures and countries I worked in, I still felt done with the game. Fortunately, it had allowed me financial success for a long time, but I was still deeply bothered by the struggles my peers and I faced in our attempts to achieve and maintain these ideals.

When I first started my career, I felt less beautiful, less empowered, and less sure of myself. On one hand, I had a sense of belonging, but on the other hand, I wasn't fully belonging to myself. I did my best to help myself and the other girls around me cope with these pressures while staying centered, but it was a lot.

Looking back, I can see that I stayed so long in that industry because of the experience I first had on my sixteenth birthday. I had so much synchronicity as I entered the modeling business that I felt it was where I was meant to be. But it didn't mean I needed to stay there forever.

But that's the thing; I have countless clients who talk about looking for signs outside of themselves or being guided externally. I want to stress the importance of understanding that the opportunities that present themselves to us are options; they aren't signs of what to do or what not to do. We aren't here to be codependent on external signs, but rather to see them as options and use our free will to decide whether that is what we want to experience.

I moved to Los Angeles at age twenty-one to sign with a major theatrical agent and begin my acting career after traveling the world for many years as an international model. While I experienced many exciting moments, I often felt like just an observer rather than an active participant. My soul didn't connect with these experiences like I thought it would.

For years, I thought this career was meant to be because of how perfectly it unfolded, totally denying my right to my own free will. I kept myself in the career for probably a decade too long just because I thought it was what I was meant to do, so if I wasn't the best at it, I was failing my purpose. This is completely incorrect thinking.

I struggled to maintain that connection to my true self for far too long. My biggest wound was the feeling that I was not measuring up to my purpose. That belief not only made it difficult for me to find a place where I belonged but also made me feel like I didn't belong to myself.

I found it hard to relate to anyone in this experience. How do you express that you're trying not to lose your true self? I longed to find other people on this journey of awakening, but whenever I spoke about it with friends or elders, they would respond with confusion.

I just wanted people to awaken so I could feel strong enough to trust my experiences. Little did I know that I was going through all of this so that one day I would be able to support and guide others to awaken to their higher truth, their divine identity. In real time, I was gaining the tools I needed to stay connected.

At that point, I had moved past the collapse phase but was still navigating the management stage.

That's the tricky part: trauma does not heal through achievement or validation from others. Many people continuously await a sign from God, but the God I eventually connected with began communicating with me through my commitment to acknowledging, expressing, and living out my most authentic feelings. Instead of trying to get things right, I focused on learning through my mistakes. The perfection I once sought would turn into me embracing the perfection of the process.

Through many years on my healing journey, I learned that life will only reflect the beliefs you hold about yourself. Things show up not to validate or invalidate you, but to reveal where you are invalidating yourself. The true awakening is when you understand that the inner work brings forth parts of you that are not yet aligned with your truth.

This is what is often referred to as "the dark night of the soul." After a decade and a half of seeking, I had my breakthrough moment, but this was also when the real work began: the embodiment and integrity that followed.

As I relay the chapters of my journey to you, I will share steps that reflect your own path.

This is a journey of embodying your truth, not just understanding it.

You are here to be the change, and that requires you to act in the name of authenticity.

As you navigate your own authentic path, I want you to find your ability to shine your light. As a result, you can become a beacon for others. It's crucial to understand that you are born perfect for your purpose, but that purpose can only be discovered when you completely let go of the need for external confirmation and start giving authority back to your inner world.

You cannot find self-validation until you free yourself from self-doubt. The world will only reflect the beliefs you hold about your worth, not the true essence of your worth. It can feel like the system is working to disempower you, but that's because most people give their power entirely to the system and demand that you do, too. But people with sensitivity are meant to be the leaders of the new paradigm, the frontrunners of change and transformation, impacting the world by first becoming aware of their truth, then living in alignment with it.

If you struggle with feeling different, please know that your uniqueness serves a purpose and is meant to make a difference. Through my journey of self-awakening and realization, I have learned that no one can heal me except myself. However, years of doubt, labeling, emotional neglect, and perfectionist ideals need to be addressed and cleared. I call this "the way of the old world versus the way of the new earth."

Once I reached the point of clearing my emotional pain, I began to trust and believe in my own wisdom. That was where my wisdom was hidden. Until we heal our wounds, we cannot access the wisdom beneath them. When clients come to me and can't find their purpose, I gently direct them into the space of their original emotional wounds.

Emotional healing is the first step; it allows us to confront and process our feelings honestly. We learn to fill the void of self-love and connect with our true divine nature. The only way to heal is to stop judging our feelings and start processing those stored experiences and misinterpretations so they can be upgraded.

Our awakening begins to anchor when we realize that we are here to heal generational traumas and break the cycle. The system is flawed, the world is hurting, and we can serve as examples of consciousness rather than as expressions of the unconscious.

For the Ones Who Came Early

You were not born too sensitive.
You were born perceptive
In a world still learning how to feel.

You noticed the cracks
Before language existed for them.
You carried questions
No one had yet learned to ask.

They called you different
Because they could not name your assignment.
But differences were never the wound—
They were the signal.

You came early
To feel what others would one day understand.
To awaken when the world was still asleep.
To hold the frequency
Of what had not yet arrived.

The new world does not begin with force.
It begins with those
Who could not harden,

Who would not numb,
Who stayed open long enough
To lead.

If you have always felt
Out of place,
Out of time,
Out of sync—

Good.
That is how pioneers arrive.

Chapter Summary

- **My Awakening and Existential Crisis:** At sixteen, the author experiences a profound spiritual awakening during a church trip that brings a sense of oneness, purpose, and freedom from the belief that she is "the problem." This moment becomes the first true mirror of her worth and divine identity.
- **The Collapse After Awakening:** Despite this breakthrough, unresolved shame and attachment wounds resurface when peer rejection triggers an intense emotional collapse. The chapter frames this as an identity crisis caused by old trauma colliding with a newly emerging self.
- **Attachment Injury and Inner Child Wounds**: A childhood breastfeeding rupture, tied to her father's affair and her mother's distress, is revealed as an early attachment injury. The author connects later rejection sensitivity, perfectionism, and fear of abandonment to this original emotional wound.

- **Perfectionism as a Survival Strategy:** In the absence of support or understanding, the author copes by becoming perfectionistic, using achievement, appearance, and popularity to avoid rejection and prove worth. This survival pattern follows her into modeling, where external validation deepens her disconnection from herself.
- **Ego Career versus Soul Calling:** The chapter distinguishes between careers pursued for validation and paths rooted in self-validated truth. The author reflects that modeling mirrored her family wounds, while her true calling emerged through healing, inner-child integration, and helping others reconnect with their authentic selves.
- **Healing as Self-Validation and Purpose:** The central lesson is that trauma does not heal through success, signs, or external approval but through emotional honesty and inner-child integration. The author reframes sensitive people as early awakeners and cycle breakers whose purpose is revealed through healing their wounds and embodying their truth.

PART 2

THE WOUNDED HEALER

CHAPTER 4

TOXIC RELATIONSHIPS: LEARNING TO SECURELY ATTACH

Sensitive souls are rarely wounded by accident; they are shaped by their environments. From an early age, many sensitive people grow up in families, cultures, and systems that do not understand how to nurture depth, intuition, or emotional truth.

When a child is perceptive, emotionally open, and intolerant of neglect or inconsistency, their surroundings often respond with misunderstanding. Over time, the sensitive child learns a painful lesson: *Who I naturally am is not safe here and not okay.* Even more distressing, they internalize the belief that they do not belong. This is where the wound forms, not because sensitivity is a flaw, but because it is unsupported and unacknowledged.

To survive, the sensitive soul adapts, developing a personality that functions in a world that values compliance, performance, and emotional suppression. However, underneath this adaptation lies an unintegrated truth, a deeper self that has not been recognized, protected, or honored.

This internal split gives rise to the wounded healer. When sensitivity is unwelcome, it does not disappear; it turns inward.

The child begins to constantly monitor their behavior, asking themselves questions like, *Am I too much? Did I do something wrong? How can I make this easier for everyone else?*

Gradually, overresponsibility replaces authenticity. The sensitive soul starts to believe there is something wrong with them and strives to compensate for it. They become hyper-aware of others' emotional states, learning to regulate their environment rather than being influenced by it.

Many clients ask me if we are born highly sensitive or if it is created by the environment. My answer is both. We are born and also shaped: born with a nervous system that feels more, notices more, and processes life more deeply, then formed by environments that don't know how to mirror or protect that depth. Many come into the world with heightened awareness, intuition, and emotional attunement, but in households marked by stress, inconsistency, criticism, or emotional absence, sensitivity quickly turns into hypervigilance.

The sensitive soul learns to scan for danger, moods, and shifts in energy as a survival skill, not because they are broken but because awareness is the safest way to stay connected and protected. Over time, this constant state of alertness can look like anxiety, ADHD, or emotional intensity when, in truth, it is a finely tuned nervous system shaped by both natural sensitivity and the need to adapt to an emotionally unpredictable world. What begins as a gift of deep perception becomes a coping mechanism until healing allows it to return to its original power.

The wounded healer learns early on that if they carry the pain, perhaps they will belong and be loved. As they mature, the wound does not vanish; instead, it evolves.

Many wounded healers find success in roles that reward attunement, adaptability, or fixing. They may excel professionally, creatively, or socially, presenting a façade of confidence. However, internally, something feels off. They often pursue paths that validate them externally but fail to nourish their inner selves. They confuse being chosen with being valued.

Ultimately, they learn to perform their worth rather than truly embody it. Although they may achieve, succeed, or be admired, they still feel ungrounded in their identity because the original wound was never about their abilities. It was about not being truly met.

As the unhealed wound begins to express itself more clearly in relationships, the dynamic becomes toxic. The original wound was relational; the one the wounded healer experiences with their family and world becomes the one they have with themselves and all others with whom they are emotionally intimate. They are often drawn to partners who resonate with their nervous system, typically those who are intense, emotionally unavailable, wounded, or inconsistent.

The nervous system I'm talking about is one that has experienced emotional neglect and lack of mirroring. When we never have the experience of being deeply seen or fully loved, we think love is intensity, chemistry is our soulmate, and the unavailable one triggers our low dopamine into earning love. The healthy one feels boring because they are not a chase. The toxic one feels intoxicating, as they are something to win.

These relationships often start with intense chemistry and a strong connection, or at least the perception of one. Initially, we feel understood, seen, helpful, and validated because we are needed. However, old patterns eventually resurface.

We begin to over-explain our feelings, minimize our needs, and take responsibility for the emotional stability, or instability, of the relationship. We start to doubt our perceptions when faced with distorted realities and engage in constant over-explanation. Gradually, we are recast as the problem, labeled as too sensitive, too emotional, or too demanding. The original wounds come to the surface.

Meanwhile, the partner avoids accountability, growth, or emotional presence, much like their original family dynamics. Unconsciously, they reenact the same patterns learned during childhood. This behavior stems not from bad judgment but rather from conditioning.

As wounded healers, we have been conditioned to tolerate emotional inconsistency and to believe that love requires endurance. Toxic relationships can feel magnetic because they mirror the original experience and carry the pain necessary for connection to survive. But they also mirror a new opportunity to shift this dynamic and say no to the old pattern.

Many of my clients worry that they are not healed enough, thinking that if they were, they wouldn't still be attracting these partners. Growth happens when we realize we will always attract such people because we are natural healers. Now, though, we have new boundaries and discernment to choose again. We recognize the signs earlier and step away faster.

I was a late bloomer and didn't have a real boyfriend until college. I now understand that intimacy was scary for me due to the huge layer of protection I had around my heart. My first boyfriend was my best friend in high school, which naturally made him the safe choice. He genuinely cared for me and was stable. That relationship was built on friendship, and if I had been ready, it would have been great. But I had other plans, and I soon found myself bored with the stability and consistency.

I framed this restlessness as a desire to explore the world. I left Chicago, our hometown, for Los Angeles to pursue my dreams of modeling and acting. He wanted to come with me, but I rejected that idea.

I was still operating under a fairy-tale narrative, one in which an exciting life and a Prince Charming would rescue me from my childhood. My blueprint was Cinderella. My first relationship after that seemed picture-perfect.

We were both cast in a new show together, and we clicked instantly. I fell in love with the image we presented as a couple, the new identity I gained from being seen as the "Barbie and Ken" pair. After all, I was still under the impression that a perfect image meant a perfect life. But I was also quickly becoming aware that the image is often the cover-up. And the reality of that situation was about to come to light.

He was ten years older than me and controlling. At the time, I registered "controlling" as "protective." He drove a cute BMW convertible and exhibited possessive behavior early on, which honestly made me feel safe. I misconstrued his possessiveness as love. At twenty-one, I was quite naïve.

Not long after we started dating, I began feeling pressure from him to comply in ways that didn't feel aligned with my inner world. I also remember thinking that I truly just wanted to be free, yet I started to feel trapped. I was modeling for major brands and gaining visibility, while he was experiencing less success. As a result, he grew increasingly controlling and, ultimately, mean.

I remember one night, in particular, I had just returned home from a big Hollywood event at the Playboy Mansion. That month, I had been featured on the cover of a huge magazine, and the magazine had sponsored my outfit and night out. I was not allowed to bring a guy with me to the mansion party because they had a strict list, so I went with a close girlfriend I had met through my modeling agency.

We had an amazing time, and I couldn't wait to share all the details with him when I got home. However, upon arriving home that evening, I was met with his rage, name-calling, and devaluation. I felt afraid of what he might do next. This had come out of nowhere.

Deciding to escape his angry mood, I started walking from his house to mine. I lived only a few blocks away, so I felt safe. But before I knew it, I heard him running after me.

He grabbed me and began shouting, blaming me for his mood and listing all the terrible things about me that made him feel out of control. The truth was that he felt this way because I had gone to the party without him, and he had no control over me in the ways he had been trying to enforce. I'd had fun like any twenty-one-year-old should, and I had also conducted myself very respectfully in the relationship.

He knew I was one of the most loyal people, and he couldn't risk that changing. He grabbed me again and pushed me. That was the first and only time I have ever been physically harmed by another person. I was in complete shock.

At that moment, my friend who had come with me to the party pulled up to the curb. I still don't know how she sensed something was off, but she did. She and her boyfriend grabbed me and took me to safety. I never heard from that guy again; he was arrested and sent to anger management for three years.

Many years later, I ran into him at another party in Los Angeles. To my surprise, he walked up to me and thanked me for helping him, admitting that he'd had issues with substance abuse and anger that I had never known about because even he had been in the dark about how serious it was.

He apologized profusely and wished me well, expressing pride in me for doing the right thing. Unfortunately, this wasn't the last time I would date someone with substance abuse issues or anger management problems.

Even though I acted correctly in that situation, it did not heal the underlying wounds that attracted me to narcissistic partners with addictions.

I was young and living in the center of Hollywood, so I attracted people who lived in an idealized world rather than the real world. These men validated me and showered me with attention as a substitute for love.

For many wounded healers, external validation can temporarily soothe the ache of not being internally anchored.

There was so much praise, success, beauty, and productivity around me that it became a stand-in for belonging. The sensitive soul may think, *If I'm admired, I won't be abandoned. If I am helpful, I won't be abandoned. If I can continue to prove my worth, I won't be abandoned.* But when you are a twenty-one-year-old in Hollywood, your worth means your beauty, talent, and how much money you bring in for your agency.

However, validation is inherently conditional, and it cannot fill a void that was never addressed.

Over time, even success started to lose its ability to satisfy my deeper needs. After I abruptly ended that toxic relationship, I moved in with an amazing woman who felt like an older sister to me. Eventually, she became very famous.

You may know her as Fergie from the Black Eyed Peas. When I first moved in, she had not yet joined the group. She was incredibly kind and made me feel really comfortable and safe. I loved living with her.

This period marked a significant turning point in my life; my career was really taking off, and so was my social circle. I was landing guest spots in nearly every sitcom I auditioned for. I had no idea how fortunate I was; I was conditioned to expect this level of success from myself to maintain my sense of worth. These unattainable perfectionistic standards were hard to deal with behind the scenes, but somehow, I did.

I was traveling frequently for work, then coming home to this cool big-sister figure I'd never had. That support, combined with my successes, helped me move on from the pain of the toxic relationship I had left behind.

I remember booking a prestigious role and feeling ecstatic that my family would finally see how great I was. I hoped that maybe they would finally be so proud that I would feel relief. Unfortunately, that never happened. I knew they were proud of me and would share my news with friends, but it never stuck with me. Instead, I developed a codependency on external validation.

When I would book a new TV spot or shoot, I felt confident and elated. But during periods of uncertainty in my career, I would sink into a deep void. I would berate myself for not having the perfect body or for not doing everything right. Somehow, I always blamed myself as the reason for the emotional void.

If I didn't get booked for a job, the doubt and uncertainty about my identity would resurface. I was on a constant roller coaster of emotion. My identity became "Candace the model and actress," rather than "Candace the *person*." Growing up as the family scapegoat meant that my identity was often defined by the roles I played. I remember thinking that I was literally trying to upgrade my role. Funny how the irony of the situation was so accurate.

What was so sad about this is that, at that young age, I was always searching for a role and had no idea there was a reality outside of that. I was either playing a character on TV, posing for a magazine image, or being some successful guy's girlfriend.

Whenever I felt unsuccessful at work, there was always a guy waiting in the wings to make me feel special. My self-worth became dependent on who I was dating or what project I was chosen for. The common theme was being "chosen."

When you've never felt chosen by your family, no amount of external validation can fill that gap. The truth is, I had not yet chosen myself. I was waiting for life's endless permission slips to confirm, validate, and secure that self-acceptance for me.

However, life can only reflect your own level of self-integration. While I worked a lot and had long-term relationships with men who adored me, it all came at a cost. When self-worth is outsourced, a collapse is inevitable.

The void emerges when that coping strategy fails. Eventually, the wounded healer reaches a breaking point, and the mechanisms that once protected them begin to cause harm.

The Void

This often manifests as emotional exhaustion, anxiety, depression, relationship collapse, loss of identity, and spiritual disorientation. I refer to this state as "the void." The void is not emptiness; it is the absence of your true self.

It emerges when the healer can no longer rely on performance, people-pleasing, or external approval to survive. This experience can feel terrifying because the old identity dissolves before the new one is formed. However, this moment is not a failure; it is an initiation. The healer's ultimate lesson is to learn to heal the self.

I was twenty-six years old. I had read a lot of spiritual books, but I still had not started walking my talk.

I had broken off an engagement to someone I'd once called "my twin flame." We had an intense relationship that opened up a whole new world for me. It started beautifully, and he courted me like no other. This man took me on the adventures of my dreams, and I felt like an absolute princess. Almost immediately, we both knew we had a purpose in each other's lives that went much deeper. We called it "karma ripening," and we were off to explore what the divine had in store for us.

For eight years, on and off, I lived a high life of what I thought was higher love with him. We always centered our spirituality and lifestyle over everything else. This was my first love! At the beginning, I kept my independence and even left L.A. to move to Miami for ten months to film a Swedish soap opera, *Ocean Avenue*. When I returned to L.A., the home he had been building that year on top of the hill was ready for us to move right in.

We had a magical few years there, traveling with his family and living our best L.A. lives. He was incredibly successful, brilliant, popular, and social. He had an amazing family, whom I adored, and we lived in our dream house on top of a hill. I did not think life could get any better than that.

I was working a lot and enjoying it, but I also willingly compromised parts of myself to fit into his world. I became comfortable in that role, and I remember feeling that my worth was finally anchored. I knew what I deserved because he showed me through our connection, lifestyle, and dreamy perceived future together. But my worth was mostly anchored to him.

However, I did not realize that what I was calling a twin flame was actually a twin to my trauma; it was a trauma bond. We both had work to do, but rather than fully addressing our issues, we got by by loving each other unconditionally, even when that love was not healthy. Looking back, it was as if our inner children needed each other to feel whole.

I allowed his unhealthy cycles to continue, and in return, he allowed me to have my emotional traumas. As time passed, I started experiencing debilitating monthly migraines and symptoms of extreme inflammation.

At the time, I was unaware that I was compromising my own power and becoming increasingly dependent on him for my safety and sense of self. My fairy-tale life felt just within reach, but I wasn't able to grasp it. When we got engaged, I felt like I had won the lottery in love and life.

I thought I was in love; I loved our life and was excited about our future. However, I realized that I loved him more than I loved myself, and he loved his party lifestyle more than he loved me.

My identity was wrapped up in his reflection of me. I had made him my false idol. I couldn't function if he was mad at me, which would lead to emotional breakdowns that manifested as physical symptoms. To cope, I focused on pleasing him as best as I could.

After our engagement, I relaxed a bit and felt confident enough in us that I revamped my modeling contracts.

I left for a trip to New Zealand and had the best time of my life because I knew I had him as my anchor. I was able to spread my wings as this more confident version of myself. However, during the trip, I realized that while I loved him deeply, I was questioning whether this was right for either of our futures. I could feel myself shifting my sense of self-worth from the relationship back to my career. My abandonment wounds also came up when I didn't hear from him for days. He was closing a big deal for his company, but I expected more communication.

My career was going extremely well overseas at this point, and it was now providing me with a sense of personal security again. I started to really reflect, and I got honest with myself about this relationship I was now engaged in. I allowed myself to see what was in plain sight: neither of us was prioritizing getting married; the priority was not losing each other. Suddenly, I could not see our future together. It was as if we'd gotten engaged because we loved each other so much, but we couldn't get married because we did not yet love ourselves.

Our engagement eventually ended, but we stayed in touch for many years until we became engaged again. I had grown during this time but still felt unanchored. He had dated around but had not been serious about anyone. Our second engagement was an attempt to save what had once been the dream, but it ended only six months later, this time for good.

We loved each other deeply, and we felt better when we were together, but neither of us knew how to truly love ourselves on our own. After the second breakup, I began experiencing panic attacks. That was always my go-to symptom when I was experiencing severe attachment trauma.

To cope with the emotional void, I started numbing more through avoidance and performative spirituality, reading a ton of books but not fully practicing the teachings. This wasn't working, though, and I realized I was going to have to do the opposite of what I had done in the past.

In my coaching practice, I call this "the counterintuitive method." Whatever feels most comfortable, don't do that. Do the things that stretch you. For the first time in my life, I actually tried to date casually instead of always having a boyfriend. I thought I was spreading my wings and exploring, but in reality, I was about to go through a major transition.

My wounds were no longer anchored in the false sense of security provided by another person or by career achievements. Instead, they were surfacing, seeking healing.

Saturn Returns

"Saturn returns" refers to the time in everyone's life when Saturn is in the exact place in their astrology chart that it was when they were born. This happens between the ages of twenty-eight and thirty-two. It is the time when we go through major changes that help align us with our truest self and purpose. This is the time of deep inner-child healing, of big events like marriage, children, moving, career change, and illness. Things happen to wake us up and send us on our destined path.

My wake-up call came a year or so after my second engagement breakup. I was living in a gorgeous condo with two friends. I felt like I was turning the page from having a man as my savior into living life on my own terms. I thrived in this situation where I had independence but also friends nearby. I started running eight miles a few times a week. My roommates would look forward to joining me on the run. I started relaxing into my own lifestyle, and I felt really good. It was at this time that my roommates and I decided to throw a Christmas party at our place. This was invite-only, and it was fancy!

A male friend of mine came and noticed I had been single for a minute. This was new for me! He asked me why, and I said, "I am waiting for the one, and until then, I am happy being single." He immediately asked me what my type was, and I briefly described the guy I saw in my mind: blonde, surfer-type, but sophisticated. I like the California guy who is not from California but who is also driven.

He showed me a picture of one of his friends and asked if I knew him. I had never seen him before. He was shocked because apparently, we had many mutual friends, and according to my friend, this guy knew everyone.

The guy in the photo he showed me was exactly my physical type. So, he sent his friend a message, and this is where the story gets interesting. He sent my photo to this mystery guy, who happened to be at dinner with a mutual acquaintance, someone I had done that Swedish soap TV show with in Miami about eight years earlier. The guy asked this mutual acquaintance about me, and the mutual acquaintance said, "She's cool and nice. Go for it."

The next day, I got a message from the mystery guy, and a week later, we were on our first date. He asked me if he could send a car for me, and I said no, I would drive. I always wanted an out just in case. I was in my independent era. The second I drove up to his house and got out of my car, he looked at me and said, "There you are."

In him, I met someone who felt like my soulmate, not a twin flame that matched my trauma but a kind soul, a kindred spirit who felt like family, the healthy kind. Our connection was instant, yet it wasn't intense. And at that moment, my single, independent era came to a close.

There were no emotional highs or games; the relationship was calm and patient, without manipulation. Honestly, this confused me, but it also gave me a sense of inner freedom I never knew existed while still making me feel safe.

We traveled the world and attended fun events together. We discovered that we'd both moved to Los Angeles in the same year and grown up in similar towns in Chicago. The similarities felt strange, not in a way that triggered my nervous system but in a life-affirming way.

After a few blissful months, I wasn't feeling like things were moving forward. I was growing restless and starting to require more safety and security in the relationship. My abandonment wounds were coming up, and I wanted to leave. I wasn't feeling claimed for some reason, and the relationship was no longer stimulating my nervous system in the way I had become accustomed to.

This guy offered me freedom when I needed it and support when it felt right. He was not driven by ego or achievements. He was something of an anomaly. He didn't find his self-worth in his significant success or through other people. He was someone who simply did his own thing and did it well. But at some point, it became scary to fall for someone and not have the security of a future. I needed the next step, and he was holding on to his independence.

Needless to say, he was shocked by my need to take a break. He had not come from a dysfunctional family and could not grasp what I was going through.

As a woman needing to feel chosen, I found that this didn't satisfy me. I tried to leave the relationship and moved to New York City for a brief period. While there, I signed with Wilhelmina Models, but this time, it was different. The influence of this guy had pushed me more into my own authenticity without me even knowing it.

This time, it wasn't just about fashion; it was also about sports and fitness modeling. I had gotten passionate about yoga, and I was booking big yoga modeling jobs right off the bat. This felt much more aligned with my reality. I had been an athlete my whole life before becoming a model.

I had grown really tired of squeezing my natural size two to four frame into a double zero. I was beginning to feel more authentic and true to myself, rather than conforming to the perfectionistic images I felt I needed to uphold. I found considerable success as a fitness and yoga model, and I was loving this new phase of my career.

I also completed my yoga teacher training while in New York City, which helped me connect with what was genuinely real for me, rather than just the ideal. For the first time, it felt validating to simply be myself and find success in that.

I started dating a high-profile guy while I was in New York. He was another Ken doll, and soon, I noticed how he needed me to fit a certain image. Having just come out of my need to fit any role, I was now bumping up against an old pattern. He wanted a Stepford wife, but I no longer wished to conform to a perfect image. I still wanted a perfect family, but I wanted to build it from an authentic place. That relationship was quick, and it made me value the work I had just done on myself. I was starting to come into my power more and more, and it was exciting.

Cinderella Becomes Wonder Woman

Cinderella was transitioning into her Wonder Woman era. I had always wanted a man to save me, but I was beginning to see that I could save myself. The more authentic I dared to be, the easier things aligned. But the old programming would still come out to play. I still needed to build my capacity to maintain this authentic way of being. My old pattern of sabotage would come up from time to time.

My scapegoat mentality was so accustomed to being the problem, the reason for issues, that I found myself repeating that pattern. My coping mechanism to leave something that was not aligned for me was to create an issue instead of just speaking up. But this was no longer working for me, either.

I was stepping into new ways of being brutally honest. I was becoming comfortable with things just ending, not because something was wrong, but because it was wrong for me.

I was still working through the feelings of being unsafe when things were going too well for too long. I started to realize that this was also why I would unconsciously pick people who had an addiction or practiced avoidance. They were always playing out some kind of drama, which made my nervous system feel safer than if there had never been any break.

I eventually moved back to Los Angeles, and of course, my cycle of recycling was on full display. The kind guy I mentioned, "Mr. Nice Guy," came back in for another try. I would go from intensity to calm. When calm was too much, I would create my own intensity within relationships. This nice guy was almost too invested in my autonomy. It felt like he wanted constant individuality within our union. This, of course, triggered my abandonment wounds once again.

When you are used to love feeling more like control and possession, the partner who encourages too much freedom in the connection can feel off. Why wasn't he making me feel secure in the ways I expected? Each time I felt unclaimed, I would experience the urge to sabotage our relationship. I was reacting to his inability to create the sense of safety for my nervous system that felt familiar.

His encouragement for me to stand on my own two feet felt threatening, traumatizing, and wrong. But let's be clear: everyone has their own wounds to heal. In my opinion, he was slightly avoidant, which would make sense for me, as I was still working through my anxious attachment. My desire for more connection scared him into pulling back.

The last thing he ever said to me was, "Go learn how to love yourself first."

And what I told him was, "Stop trying to be so independent and separate."

We both had some work to do. Little did I know this would not be the last time I would see Mr. Nice Guy.

Healing does not occur when a sensitive soul learns to help others become better. It happens when they stop abandoning themselves. Integration begins with a radical internal shift: responsibility is reclaimed, self-trust is restored, and sensitivity is reclaimed rather than suppressed. The wounded healer realizes they do not need to be needed to feel worthy, and they do not need someone else to feel safe. They need to allow themselves to be their own healer.

Eventually, we need to begin choosing relationships that feel calm, reciprocal, and grounded, rather than chaotic and intense or neglectful. We stop confusing chemistry with destiny and stop chasing potential; instead, we honor reality. That relationship needs to start with ourselves.

We are, in essence, trauma-bonded to our inner child and looking for an emotional parental figure to claim us. That parental figure can only come from reparenting ourselves. Many people delay this process because they don't want to be alone, but also because they are still searching for a permission slip from someone who can never give it. This is the loop we find ourselves in, depending on the undependable, just like our original experience.

The dependable one needs to become you. But you can't do this alone; you must call on a higher power. When reparenting begins, the nervous system often seeks a surrogate parent in romantic partners, waiting for reassurance and permission that was never received in childhood. When we replace that external search with a deeper desire to face our own pain, we can rise.

This is when healthy dynamics will no longer feel boring. Sensitivity is transformed into wisdom rather than being a burden.

I got to a point where I could not continue in my old patterns anymore. I had sabotaged several relationships and was exhausted by a career that swung my confidence up and down.

I needed to anchor myself quickly. I felt on the verge of total burnout, not from life itself, but from my internal, endless cycle of searching outside myself for the healing.

My dreams were calling to me. I wanted to finally pursue the spiritual work I had longed to do since I was thirteen, but I hadn't found an outlet for it.

From a very young age, I had wanted to be a spiritual psychologist, but that option didn't exist. I had put college on hold, and over the years, I'd pursued distance learning while traveling on my modeling contracts. But this time, I just felt I was being pushed into my true path.

Then, one day, as I was walking in Santa Monica, I looked up and saw the University of Santa Monica right in front of me.

In the window, I saw that this school offered a master's program in spiritual psychology. I ran inside and grabbed the application, asked some friends to write letters of recommendation for me, and submitted everything that week. This was my calling, and I was answering.

Weeks later, I was accepted to the school, which started a two-year deep dive into my inner work. The course was intense and necessary. During those two years, I revisited every single emotional block that I had. I addressed all the resistance within me to just allow myself to feel my own emotional truth.

This was a brutal process, but it also consistently guided me into the places that scared me the most and ultimately brought new insight. I was guided to see not only that my authentic self was not flawed but also that I was protecting myself from a deeper truth. My pain, my self-image, had been created to protect myself from the trauma, not to protect myself from my truth. This need to be perfect was my way of blocking rejection, but I was deeply rejecting my inner child in the process.

After long hours of meditation, I connected with a part of myself that felt divine and sacred, and this part of me had answers. I was reconnecting with the part of me I had met during my out-of-body experience at age sixteen. It felt like a miracle.

In one of my hour-long meditations with my inner child, I spoke to my eight-year-old self. It was not like anything I had ever experienced before. She was ecstatic to connect and had been with me all along.

The guidance she gave me on how I could heal her was extremely specific, and I got the message that I had to take the actions she suggested; there was no other way. She reminded me of my pet cat, who had died when I was eight, the age of the version of me that I was talking to. She told me that to heal this part of her, I needed to get a pet, and the picture she showed me was very detailed.

That week, I searched online for an animal in the shelters to see if I could find the one. One thing I know about inner-child work is that you must first acknowledge the inner child, then take aligned action on their requests. So, I was not going to find my new pet unless it was the essence of what she suggested.

In my meditation, it looked like she was telling me to get a white kitten. But when I saw this tiny blonde puppy online, I knew this was her. This was my Honey Bee, better known as my "soulmate dog." This little baby was the essence of unconditional love on steroids. She felt like my inner child! The love I poured into her was mirrored back perfectly.

I want to take a minute to talk about Honey Bee because not only did she change my life, but she also healed my inner child. Loving Honey Bee was like loving my inner child outside of my body for seven and a half years. Honey came with me everywhere I went, and she would sit with me during every coaching season and YouTube video I filmed. She was my healing partner.

As I started to grow comfortable with this constant feeling of love, I was also dropping the need for my coping mechanisms. I started to watch myself naturally trade in perfectionism for a new safety in what was real. I stopped coloring my hair to the perfect blonde and instead allowed my natural hair color.

I began dressing in a way that felt true to me. Instead of keeping up with the latest trends, I found comfort in a more laid-back look. I engaged in profound inner-child work for hours each day just to connect and build a consistent relationship with my inner world, which led to the deepest imaginable exploration.

I met all parts of myself and ended up healing my chronic back pain, which I now see as me stabbing myself in the back. During this period, I got engaged, then married, and began writing my first manuscript. That manuscript was the precursor to this book thirteen years ago.

From 2011 to 2013, I came home to myself in a significant way; my paradigm had shifted. I let go of superficial friends and embraced a spiritual sisterhood. I stopped performing and began feeling. After ten years of acting, I walked away just before what could have been my big break. I literally said no—I could no longer do anything that felt pressured or stressful.

I notified my agent, who thought I was insane for leaving my career at this time. The inner pull to align with my true self became stronger, which brought up a lot of resistance to letting go of my ego-based life. I held on to my modeling career for a few more years, but it started to feel like a distant thought, no longer my central focus.

During this time, I landed some of my biggest accounts, as I was truly unconcerned. I was fully engaged in my new life with my husband, four stepchildren, and my beloved dogs, Honey Bee and Bodhi. I was building a life rooted in authenticity, and I loved it.

I stopped thinking about external validation and learned to self-validate. I was living from feeling, and I felt like I was in my body. I was no longer an imposter living life through a filter. I spent time healing many misinterpretations I had about myself, life, and God. Through intense shadow work, I addressed mother, father, and generational traumas.

It was here that I discovered I was born perfect for my purpose. Society was no longer my false idol or measure of worth; instead, God became the cornerstone of my life. I realized that God had made me this way (sensitive, intuitive, and different) so I could bring forward the next level of this work. I began to see a much bigger picture, and it all made sense.

Many of the gifts I'd had as a child returned. Memories began to surface, and I experienced profound insights, becoming more psychic again. I didn't see this as strange; I viewed it as a blessing. I shared my story with friends to help them through their own situations.

An actress friend of mine had a popular YouTube channel, and she asked me to do an interview on it to talk about this work. After that episode aired, I had hundreds of emails pour in, mostly from her home country, Australia. These people were very interested in the concepts I'd spoken about, and many of them wanted to coach with me.

This opportunity prompted me to start my own channel. I had genuinely transformed my life, and everyone was watching. The shift was both physical and electrical, felt by people I hadn't talked to in years.

So many things started to shift. My former agent had seen some of my videos and noted that my voice had changed. I used to speak in a very high-pitched tone, and now it was lower and more grounded. I was finally descending into my body instead of living in my head and on the surface. For the first time in my life, I felt safe enough to talk about my insights out loud. In just a week, I grew my channel to over ten thousand subscribers.

I started booking clients daily and finally found myself in the work I was meant to do. My calling had called to me, and I listened. I built my first course and published a workbook called *Spiritual Fitness*, sharing tools and insight on how to manage emotion and end toxic patterns, as I had just done. My life was becoming my teaching.

I developed a new identity. I was no longer the lost girl searching the world for her worth. I had transformed into a healer who had healed her own life. I was now in my authentic era, embracing my new role as a stepmom, coach, author, and guide.

I practiced what I preached and broke free from the family-scapegoat identity. The wound became wisdom, not because it was necessary but because it was transformed.

This is where I, as the healer, finally came home to myself. As I continued to build my business and work with regular clients, I became busier. I began to realize that I could truly create a serious career out of this. Perhaps people really needed to hear these stories; maybe they needed the gift I had discovered to translate complex, deeper spiritual concepts into easy understandings. The world seemed ready to get deeper answers that traditional therapy couldn't reach.

I started to believe in myself, not in my looks or my image, but in the truth of what I brought forward. I was now living from the inside out. As this happened, I let go of living an image-based life. I no longer cared about how things looked, how much money I had, or what I could show for it. I didn't need to prove to my family or the world that there was nothing wrong with me. The joy I felt daily and the purpose I was now living were my proof.

I became comfortable with authenticity, embracing the idea of doing things differently and not fitting in anywhere. Magically, as I did, I began to feel like I belonged everywhere. I forged connections with many different groups of friends and found my place in the world by landing in my own heart and the purpose of service.

The Initiation

Those years were deeply transformative in many ways. But here is the part no one talks about. As my external world began to reflect my newfound empowerment, my marriage began to undergo its own shifts. I was seeing cracks in what was once a solid foundation. Of course, this scared me, and the thought of my marriage ending was devastating. But marriage is tricky because there are two people on two different paths, trying to merge their lives together and grow in the same direction.

I had grown a lot since we'd gotten married, and my career was also on the rise. The roles were shifting, and the responsibilities were changing. The vision I had for my future was starting to look a little foggy. My husband had his own personal challenges with four growing children and work stress.

I was feeling capable now because I was securely attached to myself. Other people were no longer my false idols; now I was with God. I believe my success began to threaten the marriage, as hidden lies that had sustained the false image began to surface. I realized I could no longer be in a marriage where I embraced truth while my partner lived in denial.

I started to see the external structure of my life breaking down, and it felt devastating and oddly liberating rather than life-defining. I began to notice the truths about the family unit that I had never been shown or told about. As we ask for the deepest truth about ourselves, we will also see it in all things. At that moment, our house was breaking down. I stuck it out through really hard times as best as I could until the universe threw us a massive sign.

A fire in Malibu took our house, and we were forced to temporarily move to another state. Shortly after that, my beloved soulmate dog was diagnosed with cancer, and she wouldn't survive it. This took priority over the chaos of the marriage and the move away from my friends. This dog was my child, and I did everything possible to save her. This cancer came out of nowhere. She started coughing one morning, and I felt that something was very wrong. To anyone else, she looked like a dog just having an allergy. But I had a sinking feeling in my chest.

Even though my husband thought I was overreacting, I took her to the emergency vet because it was a Saturday and the regular vet was closed. I was hoping they would tell me I was overreacting, but instead, they took Honey back to get examined. A few minutes later, they asked me to come into a room and sit down to wait for the doctor.

The doctor walked in and told me that Honey had just collapsed. They said they got her back and put her on an IV. I was in shock at that point, but it got worse. Another doctor came in to explain to me that Honey had a tumor in her heart that was too big to operate on and that she might not make it through the night.

That was the first time I ever fainted; my body was in complete shock. I kept asking for more people to come in and explain the situation to me because I did not believe what they were saying. They assured me that Honey needed to stay the night, and they were not sure if I would ever see her again.

That night was the longest of my life. Honey made it through the night and stayed another night to get fluids. Thankfully, she was able to come home after that, and we made an appointment with an oncologist. The oncologist told us that Honey Bee had hemangiosarcoma.

I did more research on this than anything in my life. I was trying to understand how a perfectly healthy dog could just collapse without warning. But that is the insanity of this disease: no signs, usually, until it is almost too late.

As I was wrapping my mind around this, I was also preparing for the worst. Each day, I would look into more alternative therapies and ways to try to shrink her tumor, as it was too big to operate on. Honey Bee was an Italian greyhound, terrier, and Chihuahua mix and was only eleven pounds. She was very dainty and delicate, so surgery was out of the question.

We decided on chemotherapy and medicinal mushrooms. We were with her day in and day out. After her second chemo treatment, she was doing much better. I saw the light in her eyes coming back. I wanted to cancel the final chemo treatment and go all in on the alternatives, but I was advised that no matter what we did, we were on borrowed time.

For those six weeks, I did not leave the house. Every meal was delivered, and I took client calls from wherever Honey was lying. She had always been a fixture in my coaching sessions, so thankfully, all of my clients were as invested in her as I was.

Honey Bee taught me to truly take care of myself in all ways, so that is what I was going to do for her until her last breath. She was, after all, my inner child outside of my body. At the time, I was wavering between wanting to have my own children and not wanting them, and I would always say I didn't feel the need for that because Honey was my soul baby.

Honey Bee had her last chemo treatment, and when we got her from the hospital, I knew she was tired; she had had enough. That night, she started bleeding out. You could see the blood around her heart through her skin. I held her, made her her favorite meal, and just talked to her for hours. I thanked her for healing me and being the angel I always needed.

This part will sound strange to you, but I want to share it. That evening was the twenty-first of September. As I was holding her and my husband was calling to see if there was a vet who could come over in case we needed to put her down, she told me no. Needless to say, there was no one available to come to the house that night, and Honey Bee told me she was going to pass away the next day, on the twenty-second. I asked her why, and she said because my husband, my stepson, who was with us, and I were all born on the twenty-second, and that was her way of being a part of us forever.

At 5:55 a.m. on the twenty-second, Honey Bee let me know it was time. She tried her best to crawl up my leg while I was sleeping. I felt her and woke up to hold her. I held her in my arms for many minutes and sang all of her songs to her. Her breathing got louder, and she started to slip away in my arms. It was one of the most painful and beautiful experiences of my life. I got to send my baby off to heaven so lovingly, so meaningfully, so gracefully.

Do you remember the story I told you about how my eight-year-old inner child told me to get her? Honey Bee ended up dying just days before her eighth birthday. I saw all the connections. I was broken, but at the same time, I was strong enough to see into her higher calling.

Shortly after Honey Bee died in my arms, I needed to distance myself from the situation and my failing marriage.

I separated from my husband for four months to figure out what to do next. During that time, I created my most successful online course, "Emotional Rehab," which encompassed everything I had been through and learned up until that point. It was as if Honey Bee were now acting as my business partner from above, but even stronger. This course revealed so much of my journey and the healing principles I had created from it.

I returned to my husband to try again because I truly didn't want to lose the family I'd longed for. I was doing so well at work, and I wanted to save my family, too.

Ultimately, however, it was revealed that I needed to get a divorce.

This was the last thing I wanted to do, as this entire experience mirrored one of the most traumatic experiences I'd had in my childhood. When my parents divorced, we lost our home to a flood, and my cat died, forcing us to move. It was the same sequence of events.

I was revisiting trauma, loss, and abandonment all at once, but this time from a secure place within myself. I was losing my family, my beloved dog, my home, and everything as I knew it to be. But this time, I was integrated with my inner child thanks to Honey.

I went through with the divorce. What happened next was profound: I became my own savior.

I realized I was more capable and more successful than I had ever been. I understood that I didn't need to be defined by the perfect image of life or the ideal family. I was now living from a different consciousness. The one I was born with and the one I had worked so hard to heal back to. I had found my purpose, and I had created my own security. I had learned to love and never abandon myself.

This was my time to really lean on God. Right before the divorce went through, I went outside and asked Honey Bee's spirit if it was okay for me to get a new dog. I felt she had guided me into my empowerment, but I was still mourning her deeply. I needed a protector of this new structure I was about to live in. Me, God, my purpose, and my dog. At that moment, I looked up in the sky, and there was a double rainbow directly over my pool. I knew that Honey Bee had crossed the rainbow bridge. Then, when I asked her if this was her confirmation, it started to drizzle.

A few months later, my new pup, Saint, arrived. Saint was a little rebel, a mini golden doodle with an attitude. He immediately had a strong will and was a protector; he was my perfect little counterpart to go off and live on my own.

Honey Bee had been the embodiment of my delicate, sweet, super-feminine inner child. Saint was my strong-willed counterpart. Seeing how these animals show up exactly as we need for the shifts in our lives was incredible. Saint was the yang to Honey Bee's yin. As I entered my new chapter as a divorced CEO, he was the perfect baby for the job.

So, Saint and I moved out into our own place. The divorce took about eight months to be finalized. During that time, I made some new friends and went on some new adventures. I was sad and grieving the family I had separated from, but I felt liberated to live on my own terms.

But here's where the story takes an interesting turn. Remember the nice guy I dated all those years ago? Mr. Nice Guy? We had zero contact for a decade, and one random evening, I received an email from him. He had no idea about my divorce because I had kept that very private. He was reaching out to offer his condolences; he had heard about Honey Bee's passing, and he knew, through social media, that she had been my soulmate.

We hadn't been in contact and hadn't followed each other on any social media, and I had no idea what had happened to him. He expressed his condolences and said he was there for me as a friend, also adding that he hoped my husband was doing well, too.

Like I said, he had no idea that I was divorced. *"Funny enough,"* I wrote back, *"there is no husband anymore, but how are you?"*

Our friendship continued online for quite a while. I was in Las Vegas, and he had moved from L.A. to Atlanta to help take care of his dad, who was sick. One day, he emailed me and mentioned he would be in my area for the opening of a new hotel. We had still never spoken on the phone.

He said it would be wonderful to see me if I were available. "Yes," I replied. "Let's do that." That night, he sent a car to pick me up just as he had suggested on our very first date eleven years before.

I arrived at the hotel unsure of what to expect, but I was looking forward to seeing an old friend. When we met, it was like no time had passed. We actually ditched the event and went to have dinner instead. We talked and talked for hours, discussing our history and having some laughs; it was nice. He said, "I told you to go learn to love yourself, and wow, you really exceeded my expectations. You're healing lives now."

At that moment, it felt like we were in a completely different universe. How is it that we hadn't talked for ten years? I had done all the work, yet he was the one coming back into my life.

He hadn't gotten married or had children. He told me, "No one has ever compared to you." He had used his time to climb mountains, travel the world, race cars, and build up his business.

I share this story because I often tell my clients that their wounds aren't barriers to their truth. In fact, those wounds can lead them to their truth. We cannot miss what is meant for us.

Needless to say, Mr. Nice Guy and I felt we had unfinished business. Even though he had been living in Atlanta, he soon came to live with Saint and me.

Cinderella was the cover story. Wonder Woman is the main character.

Chapter Summary

- **The Wounded Healer and Relational Conditioning:** Sensitive people who grow up unsupported often learn to abandon authenticity in order to maintain connection and safety. This creates the "wounded healer," someone who becomes hyper-attuned to others, overresponsible in relationships, and disconnected from their own emotional truth.
- **Why Toxic Love Feels Familiar:** The chapter explains that unhealed attachment wounds draw sensitive people toward intense, inconsistent, or emotionally unavailable partners because those dynamics mirror early experiences of neglect and instability. What feels like chemistry or destiny is often a reenactment of childhood conditioning rather than secure love.
- **The Void as an Initiation:** When external validation, achievement, and romantic attachment stop working as coping strategies, the author enters "the void," a period of emotional collapse, anxiety, and loss of identity.

Rather than failure, this void is framed as an initiation into deeper healing and self-reclamation.

- **Secure Attachment Begins Within:** Healing begins when the author stops looking to partners, success, or image for worth and begins reparenting herself through inner-child work, spiritual psychology, and radical self-honesty. The core lesson is that secure attachment cannot come from being chosen by others; it must be built through self-trust, self-validation, and connection to a higher power.
- **Authenticity Over Performance:** As she sheds perfectionism, image-based living, and externally defined roles, the author reconnects with her true self and spiritual gifts. This shift transforms her life and career, moving her from a model/actress seeking approval into a healer, teacher, and guide living from inner alignment.
- **Loss, Reinvention, and Becoming Her Own Savior:** Through the loss of her marriage, home, and beloved dog, the author revisits old trauma from a more secure inner foundation and chooses not to abandon herself. The chapter ends with her stepping fully into self-led adulthood, trusting that what is truly meant for her will return from a place of authenticity rather than wounded attachment.

CHAPTER 5

CYCLE BREAKER

"Do you always have to have a purpose? Do you always have to be so serious? Can't you ever do things without reason, just like everyone else? No."

– Ayn Rand, The Fountainhead

Some souls are born unable to be small, casual, or numb to life. They struggle to play along with systems that feel hollow, dishonest, or dead. These are the sensitive souls, the scapegoats, and the cycle breakers.

They are often told they are too much, too serious, too intense, too perceptive. What others label as intensity is simply presence. What others call sensitivity is energetic clarity. What people resist is not the cycle breaker's personality; it's the frequency they carry.

There is a way to instantly recognize a cycle breaker. It's not mystical; it's relational. When a cycle breaker looks at you, you feel seen, not just observed or judged, but truly seen. Sensitive souls don't merely look at people; they look through them.

They perceive essences before personalities and truth before stories. This is why people are drawn to them without knowing why, while others feel deeply unsettled in their presence. The cycle breaker does not soothe illusions; they disrupt them.

This is not accidental; it is the reason you are here. Cycle breakers carry a warrior frequency, not the kind that seeks domination but the kind that refuses falsehood.

This energy was never intended to harm people; rather, it was meant to dismantle systems that no longer serve life. However, when this energy infiltrates unconscious systems, it can become volatile. Loving an awakened soul may feel intoxicating at first, offering depth, truth, intimacy, and emotional availability, but without awareness, these relationships can become painful.

A sensitive soul acts as a living mirror, reflecting not who people wish to be but what they have yet to heal. Unintegrated wounds rise to the surface in their presence. Shadows ignite, denial collapses, and many partners, unwilling to confront themselves, project their discomfort onto the sensitive soul, labeling them as dramatic, needy, unstable, or impossible to please.

Sensitive souls feel what society suppresses; they often articulate what the environment cannot bear. They become emotional lightning rods, not because of instability, but because they are attuned to the truth. This is why many scapegoats are accused of creating emotional climates that they did not initiate.

It's also why they are often misdiagnosed, pathologized, or told that they are the problem. In families, relationships, and even society at large, it's easier to label the truth teller as disordered than to confront the underlying disordered system itself.

However, the old layers of self-doubt can ultimately become a doorway to awakening.

From Programming to Spiritual Authority

Sensitive souls are born with a direct connection to their inner knowing. Intuition is not something they develop; it is something they learn not to abandon. Societal programming trains us to outsource our authority to parents, institutions, and partners, and to rely on systems of achievement and validation.

This is the original wound, when we first feel wrong and disconnected from self and ultimately God. This is when other people, societal standards, and other people's opinions become our God.

Cycle breakers, however, are wired differently. The friction they feel with authority is not mere rebellion but actually misalignment. They are here to remember something ancient and radical.

I remember never feeling respected by my teachers and never fully respecting them unless I felt they liked me or were being honest with me. Every effort to respect or defer to authority fell flat. I struggled to find someone I could look up to, a person who could reach the depths of what I felt and serve as a safe mirror. Unfortunately, that person never appeared.

Truth does not stem from hierarchy; it arises from coherence. As long as you seek permission, safety, or worth from others, your gifts will remain distorted. When you begin to trust your inner authority, your perception, knowing, and timing, everything reorganizes around that truth. This is when spiritual authority supplants societal conditioning.

But you may find yourself living in between worlds: the ideal versus the real.

Ideal versus Real

Cycle breakers often navigate two realities: the world as it is and the world as it should or could be. This creates profound grief, confusion, and loneliness, especially in childhood. We envision possibilities long before others are ready to acknowledge them.

We feel the gap between truth and performance, intimacy and convenience, meaning and productivity. Initially, this may seem like a flaw, but later, we recognize it as our assignment. We were never meant to fit into the old paradigm; we were meant to outgrow it and eventually embody something new. This is the time we need to really ask ourselves: *Is this ideal, or is this real for me?*

Intuition, sensitivity, and understanding of boundaries are critical. Highly sensitive people process heightened perceptions and possess acute awareness.

We read energy, tone, absence, and incongruence, and words become secondary. Often, we lack the language to express these feelings. While this sensitivity is a gift, it can become a burden without proper boundaries. Our purpose is not to carry what others refuse to feel; rather, it is to feel deeply without self-abandonment.

True mastery occurs when sensitivity and sovereignty meet, leading to peace with our mission. We are not here to fix anyone; we are here to model higher consciousness.

Our role is to show what happens when someone lives aligned with their inner truth. We demonstrate that emotional honesty, embodiment, and spiritual authority are not luxuries; they are necessities for the next paradigm of consciousness. Instead of forcing change, we become it.

This realization prompts us to leave toxic relationships, abandon unsatisfying jobs, and distance ourselves from toxic family members. It empowers us to challenge the narrative we were taught and create a life of alignment.

Ultimately, we come to understand that the only thing that ever felt wrong was the belief that there was something wrong with us, and then we remember why we are here.

To integrate this understanding, follow these steps for reclaiming your authority:

1. Write down three moments in your life when you were labeled "too much," "the problem," or "difficult."
2. For each moment, ask yourself: *What truth was I expressing or sensing that others resisted or denied?*
3. Complete the following without editing: If I fully trusted my perception, I would stop *(what?)*. If I already knew I was worthy, I would do *(what?)*. If I truly understood that there is nothing wrong with me, I would feel *(what?)*.
4. Set one boundary this week that honors your sensitivity and your truth without the need to explain or justify it. Here are some examples of what those boundaries could be:
    - Saying no when you feel pressured to say yes.
    - Not answering the phone when a toxic family member calls and not feeling guilty about it.
    - Not feeling the need to explain your choices or actions.

- Allowing yourself to have a negative reaction when someone hurts you, without apologizing for it.

Remember, sensitivity without sovereignty can lead to burnout. However, sensitivity combined with sovereignty can create leadership.

My family dynamic was very traumatizing for me. Earlier in this book, I shared that I was a diagnosed patient and scapegoated for it. I want to discuss my journey toward breaking toxic systems within my own family. It took decades for the shift to occur, but now that it has, I know it was all worth it.

For most of my youth and young adulthood, I carried the scapegoat role. I was diagnosed with ADHD at age seven, and my parents divorced when I was eleven. I struggled to find a balance between living with my mom and visiting my dad whenever I could.

I felt I could relax at my dad's house. Although he was not emotionally available, he was also not controlling or demanding of me, so I was able to spread my wings and let my nervous system unwind a bit. When I was about twelve years old, my dad had a girlfriend named Katie, whom I loved. She was fifteen years younger than him and was really cool.

Katie introduced me to spirituality because she was a healer and recognized that in me. I would tell her about the lucid dreams I was having, which carried messages. She encouraged me to draw my dreams in the mornings.

She set up an easel for me, and I started drawing immediately. One of my first drawings was of a dolphin flying in the sky, with me as a spiritual princess riding on its back. I remember thinking that in the dream, I was wise and carrying a message of insight for the world below.

A couple of years later, she gave me a book called *Living Yoga* by Christy Turlington. At that time, Turlington was a famous supermodel who had found her truth through yoga. I related to this so much; I felt I was discovering my true self through the spiritual practices I was being introduced to at that young age, and I resonated deeply with them.

I had finally found a place where I truly fit, one that did not judge me but supported my personal growth. Katie helped me discover more about who I really was. When I was at my dad's house, I felt safe and had the freedom to explore my identity in nonlinear ways.

During those weekends, I didn't take my Ritalin. Dad would flush it down the toilet and insist that I didn't need it because it was the weekend and I wasn't doing homework.

When I returned to my mom's house, she often commented on how relaxed I looked and asked what I had done while I was at Dad's. I told her I just did what I wanted, usually making art, reading books, and exploring spiritual concepts.

By the time I was a teenager, I saw Dad less often. He lived a state away, and I was busy with my social life. Mom had a serious boyfriend who lived with us, but I didn't really talk to them, either; they kept to themselves, leaving me to feel alone much of the time.

My older sister and I were never close. We had different interests, and many years later, we learned that she had been caught up in a narrative that painted me as the problem child. I think she distanced herself from me to avoid potential conflict arising from that perception.

I was often told how different we were, which made it seem pointless to try to connect. Looking back, it strikes me as odd to feel that about my own sibling, especially since we were only four years apart. She was older and had her own life with dating and activities, while I was navigating the challenges of being a teenager in high school.

Though we were aware of each other's lives, we lacked the closeness you would typically expect from sisters. There was always an unspoken separation that we never addressed until many years later. When I had my awakening and then went off to Japan to model, followed by college, we hardly saw each other, and I barely interacted with my parents.

Later, I moved from Chicago to Los Angeles, where I would see my mom only during holidays or occasional visits. I saw my sister almost never, and I only spoke to my father over the phone once in a blue moon. Family meant everything to me, so this distance was heartbreaking. Eventually, I couldn't afford to visit during the holidays or figure out how to manage to see everyone when I did fly in. As a result, my boyfriend became my family, and I spent the holidays with his relatives.

Throughout my twenties, I tried to prove my worth to my family while also feeling aware of the stories that might still be circulating about me, which likely contributed to our distance. Now, instead of being the problem child, I was seen as the one who was different for having moved away and begun an exciting life in another state. The narrative had shifted slightly, but it still left a gap between the rest of my family and me.

When I was in my early twenties, my sister got married and had a baby. She had another baby just ten months later, so I became an aunt twice within less than two years. I was so excited to welcome my new nephew and niece. However, they lived far away, and I barely got to see them, although we stayed in touch.

When I was in my early thirties, I got married. This marked another upgrade in my identity: I became a wife to a very successful man, as well as a stepmom.

I was living a luxurious life in Malibu, California, and I wanted to share that experience with them. However, that was when a huge rift occurred. I invited everyone to my wedding, but no one attended except for my mom and stepdad. I couldn't figure out why. I had asked my sister to be my maid of honor, as I had been hers at her wedding. Initially, she was excited. My niece was to be a junior bridesmaid, and my nephew would stand up as well.

I knew they were getting their dresses made and their tuxes fitted, but one day, out of the blue, they decided not to come. They didn't give me any explanation that made any sense. That was in 2013, and I didn't see my niece or nephew again until twelve years later, when more of the truth surfaced.

Do you remember the story I told you about my "come-to-Jesus moment" with my mother in 2018? Well, something shifted in the family dynamic after that. I was still distant from my sister and her family, but my mother and I had grown much closer.

In 2023, my boyfriend and I moved to a mountain house near Atlanta, Georgia. He wanted to be close to his mother, and I was aware that the majority of my family also now lived between Florida and South Carolina.

One random day in 2024, my brother-in-law called me. He said he needed me to reconnect with my sister, as she really needed my support at that time. I said I was open to it, admitting I honestly had no idea why we had stopped talking in the first place. He explained that he knew why and that it needed to change.

My sister and brother-in-law came over to my house, and after not seeing each other for over a decade, we sat in my living room together with my boyfriend for seven hours and discussed everything.

We talked about why we were never close and how that was confusing to all of us. They told me how proud they were of me, how they had begun to see through the lies told about me, and how wrong they had been. They shared the struggles they had had with our parents and expressed deep regret for the time wasted not being in each other's lives. My identity was transforming before my eyes.

I asked them why I hadn't been allowed to see their kids for so long. They explained that they just never knew what was true or what was a lie, and the kids had stayed away because it wasn't discussed. This is a common issue in emotionally wounded families. Nothing is ever openly talked about; there's a lack of transparency and honesty.

After those seven hours, we all felt much better. We cried, shared stories, and talked about our upbringing and lives. They shed new light on their own struggles and their strained relationship with our parents, which I didn't expect. I began to realize that no one in a dysfunctional family escapes unscathed.

My sister had endured her own traumas, and she was very clear that she had not been spared from the effects of the family system, either. I might have been a scapegoat, but she was equally wounded by it all.

The following week, I received a call from my niece, whom I had not seen since she was twelve. Now twenty-four, she wanted to come visit me, and I was thrilled about it. I was seeing the perfection of life's process. I'd divorced, gotten back together with Mr. Nice Guy, and moved across the country with him to Atlanta, and now I was reconnecting with my family while having an identity upgrade.

A few days later, my niece came over with one of her best friends. She asked me to help her get ready for a concert nearby. We talked for hours and made plans to see each other again.

She was now old enough to understand many things on her own, so we discussed our family dynamics together. I learned that her upbringing had been far from perfect as well. The generational trauma had continued in some ways. However, she was strong and smart, and she had support and had always been best friends with her little brother.

That year, the two of them spent Thanksgiving at my house, and we also celebrated Christmas together. The bond I have been able to create with them after all these years is something one can only dream of. She feels like the daughter I never had, and my nephew has turned into an incredible young man.

This part of healing is something I would never have imagined in a million years. My niece is now on her own healing journey and has found writing poetry to be her outlet.

As we heal and reject the roles we were once assigned, the truth can come to the surface, and those who can see through the lies will find it, too.

I feel like I have regained much of my family in the last few years. They now seem to see me as the healed one, the guide, the cycle breaker, rather than the problem child. Such a shift is not always the case, but it is absolutely possible.

Not everyone will come around, but it's important to stay on the path to your sovereignty. In the last year or so, I have taken many trips with my niece, and we have been making up for lost time. I have had talks with my sister, and it has been really nice. My Mom has come to visit us in the mountains, and our families have met. The best part of healing myself is that my life has become an open invitation to healing for all who enter it.

It is not about healing so that others see you; it is about healing so that you can clearly see yourself and live a life that attracts love and welcomes abundance in all forms. Miracles become a regular occurrence, and opportunities find you when you stay open to what is real, honest, and a mirror to your soul.

My niece wrote a beautiful poem for my birthday this year, and I want to share it with you. It tells the story of our reunion and brings profound healing to my heart.

Here is Jessica's poem:

My Beacon of Light

Twelve years later, part of my soul returns to me in the form of my aunt, a person I was forbidden to connect with for reasons still unknown to both of us. Instead of constantly pondering the reasons, we use this time to rebuild what was once lost. We laugh, cry, smile, and talk for hours. She takes me on new adventures, and I show her what family love is supposed to look like.

We bask in the love we share and protect our peace together. We hold each other's hands while traveling difficult roads, side by side, speaking our devastating truths while empowering one another. My aunt and I have plans, and the most important one is to never let each other feel alone again, to always be present in each other's lives.

We have found each other again after twelve years, over 4,380 long days. Our souls are whole again, and our hearts have found a missing piece in each other. In her, I have found hope; she is my beacon of light, shining brightly in my once darkest sky. She is my greatest gift, my northern star, leading me to peace.

I love you, Aunt Candy.

Chapter Summary

- **The Cycle Breaker as Truth-Teller:** The chapter defines cycle breakers as sensitive souls who cannot conform to false, emotionally dead, or misaligned systems. Their intensity is reframed as presence, their sensitivity as clarity, and their purpose as disrupting denial rather than soothing it.
- **From External Programming to Inner Authority:** Sensitive people are often conditioned to outsource worth and truth to parents, institutions, and relationships. Healing begins when they reclaim spiritual authority, trust their inner knowing, and stop treating external validation as the final measure of who they are.
- **Sensitivity Plus Sovereignty:** The chapter emphasizes that sensitivity alone can lead to burnout, but sensitivity joined with boundaries and self-trust becomes

leadership. Cycle breakers are not here to carry everyone else's pain, but to model emotional honesty, discernment, and a new way of living.

- **Breaking the Family Narrative:** The chapter shows how decades of scapegoating, distance, and false narratives within the author's family slowly began to unravel. As she healed and refused the old identity, family members eventually started to see her not as the problem child, but as the one who had been telling the truth all along.
- **Healing Changes the Whole System:** The author's reconnection with her sister, niece, and nephew demonstrates that when one person exits a false role, the larger family system can begin to shift. While not every relationship is repaired, healing creates the conditions for truth, reconciliation, and more authentic connection to emerge.
- **Sovereignty Opens the Door to Love and Abundance:** The core message of the chapter is that healing is not about finally getting others to approve of you, but about seeing yourself clearly and living from that truth. When cycle breakers reclaim their authority, they stop chasing belonging and instead create a life that naturally attracts aligned relationships, purpose, and abundance.

CHAPTER 6

SPIRITUAL DIS-EASE

We are not human beings having a spiritual experience. We are spiritual beings having a human experience."

—Pierre Teilhard de Chardin

When the body bears the cost of betraying the self, there comes a moment, often long before physical symptoms appear, when it begins to protest a life that is not true. This protest is rarely sudden; it starts quietly and subtly and is often easy to dismiss. It may manifest as fatigue, anxiety, depressive feelings, or a sense of being off, disconnected, or hollow.

For a sensitive soul who spends years overriding their intuition, suppressing their truth, and contorting themselves to fit into systems that reject their nature, the body eventually finds a way to express what the voice has been silenced from saying. This is not a sign of pathology; it is a manifestation of spiritual dis-ease. Spiritual dis-ease is not a failure of the body; it is the body's response to prolonged self-betrayal.

When you go against your authentic nature for long enough, silencing your perceptions, muting your needs, swallowing your truths, tolerating misalignment, and lacking a world that reflects who you truly are, your nervous system remains in a chronic state of threat. The body was never designed to live in constant override. For sensitive souls, the cost of this is often much higher.

The scapegoat who has endured toxic relationships and acted as a cycle breaker may feel incongruence immediately. You sense emotional dishonesty, relational imbalances, and energetic misalignments. Over time, all of this negativity can accumulate in your body.

Eventually, your body can no longer bear the burden and turns against you. This is not about being weak or unaware; it is simply a biological response.

Our bodies reflect how we operate. When our survival depends on compliance within our families, relationships, or societal systems, we learn to ignore the signals our bodies are sending us. As a result, the body keeps the score.

Symptoms as Regulation

Over time, this internal conflict manifests in many different ways. Over the last thirteen years, I have seen very specific coping mechanisms in my clients. One of the most common is eating disorders.

Disordered eating can show up in many forms, like anorexia, bulimia, or binge eating, reflecting attempts to reclaim control, disappear, or purify by overriding the body's needs.

Many clients who have experienced issues around food also note that they felt in constant battle or misalignment with their surroundings. Autoimmune conditions can develop, with the body turning against itself after years of self-attack and suppression. Chronic fatigue, fibromyalgia, and autoimmune and pain syndromes can occur as the nervous system collapses after prolonged hypervigilance.

Anxiety and panic disorders may arise, representing intuition without agency. Depression, which I call "repression of self," can be seen as grief turned inward when expression feels unsafe. These are not random occurrences; rather, they are just a few examples of the repercussions of spiritual dis-ease.

These are logical outcomes of living in opposition to one's truth. When sensitive people are made to feel inadequate or inherently flawed, despair can take hold. This goes beyond mere disappointment, becoming a deep sense of failure, as if they have betrayed their life's purpose. This can lead to depression, anger, neurotic behavior, and even self-destructive tendencies.

The weight of feeling that your purpose is lost can be incredibly heavy. Research shows a connection between eating disorders and neurodivergence. Some studies suggest that neurodivergent individuals may experience differences in brain chemistry, such as serotonin imbalances, which can lead to food restriction or overconsumption as a means of self-medication or self-regulation.

From my own experience with perfectionism, I have gained insight into this painful dynamic. I used perfectionism as a way to delay or isolate myself from further abandonment or rejection. However, the act of controlling ourselves is, in itself, a form of self-abandonment.

I recall the moment when self-abandonment took hold of me, leading me to cope with the constant threat of rejection from the world. At that time, self-abandonment felt safer than the weight of failing at my own purpose. However, when we abandon ourselves, we begin to exist in a world of proving ourselves and performing for others, losing touch with our purpose.

Eating disorders often emerge when sensitive souls internalize a narrative of failure based on society's harsh standards. This struggle to find a sense of belonging or divine connection in the world can lead to feelings of isolation and despair.

Some people may unconsciously self-sabotage because they believe they do not deserve to live fully engaged lives unless they can express themselves perfectly and be unconditionally loved. I refer to this as "spiritual perfectionism." Many sensitive souls experience this because they are aware of their sensitivity but feel helpless to prove it.

When I began my modeling career, I was terrified of failure. That fear was amplified by the feelings of rejection and inadequacy I had carried since childhood. In my teens, I believed that achieving perfection according to society's standards would protect me from rejection. It sounds extreme now, but that was how I thought back then. I was convinced that safety, acceptance, and belonging depended entirely on being the perfect version of myself.

Earlier, I shared how my experience with Ritalin led to what I would call drug-induced anorexia, underscoring the intensity of this struggle. I lost too much weight before my contract in Japan began. My agent told me they wanted me to be my natural self.

That experience taught me a fundamental truth: we never feel safe when we live according to others' standards, societal measures, or perfectionistic ideals. True safety and freedom come when we align with our own sense of what is good and right for our well-being.

You will be tested to see if you are still conforming or going against the system to preserve your sense of self. After many years of trying to earn love and acceptance, I broke my body down to the point where I had no choice but to turn away from others' opinions and toward my body's own wisdom. The joy that arose from honoring my unique mind, body, and soul was unmatched.

However, this message does not always resonate with a mind that has been conditioned to feel wrong, different, or inadequate in some way. Mastery, not perfection, is the goal. I had to learn hard lessons about self-acceptance, regardless of who agreed with me.

When we give ourselves what we truly need, rather than what we think we should need, alignment naturally flows. This is the time we turn all the "shoulds" into "coulds." Our minds have become adept at knowing what we should want to be accepted, what we should eat to have the perfect body, and how we should exercise to achieve a physical goal.

However, when we live by those "shoulds" that aren't right for us, our bodies let us know. The body is not the enemy of spiritual growth; it is the messenger. When you listen early, it whispers. When you ignore it, it screams. But when you truly align, the body becomes a partner again. You don't have to force healing; you simply need to stop violating your nature.

You were not meant to survive at the cost of yourself. Your body may break the rules so your soul can come home. Spiritual dis-ease is not the end of the story; it's the point where your truth becomes non-negotiable. From this point forward, healing does not come from fitting in; it comes from standing in alignment, no matter who feels uncomfortable.

When our nervous systems finally start to relax, old patterns come to the surface. For me, it was when I got married, and I finally felt like I was in a healthy relationship; I had a safe place to land. My husband was invested in my desire to shift from a modeling career to the calling of being a spiritual coach and teacher.

He understood that I needed time to move out of survival mode, and he was very supportive in helping me do so. I remember him telling me to just relax. If I wanted to go to school, he supported that. If I wanted to retire from modeling and acting, that was fine, too. I had the space and time to reorganize my life and my nervous system.

I remember how hard I used to be on myself. I had strict rules about how much I needed to work out and how I needed to limit my sugar intake, among other things. But I would often rebel against my own rules. My friends would always laugh at how I would talk about needing to be good for my upcoming photoshoot while shoving my face full of licorice.

I would stress about these expectations, but I was also already rebelling against them. When I first got married, my husband would gently suggest, "Honey, why don't you just stay home and relax today? Maybe do some of your writing and go for a hike, whatever you feel like." The idea of not feeling pressured to always perform, achieve, or produce something was foreign to me, yet it felt amazing.

This man loved me for who I was. He didn't care about what I accomplished or how much money I was making. He simply wanted me to be happy and to feel good.

I remember looking in the mirror one day and asking myself what the pressure was really about. Why did I feel this constant need to be perfect and adhere to rigid rules? The answer was that I didn't want to be the reason something didn't work out.

I hear this a lot with my clients. They are so used to making themselves the reason they didn't get the love they needed, or the reason the toxic guy was toxic. The self-blaming game can be loud, and at this point in my life, I was ending that cycle.

I recognized that this need to be perfect was a way to convince myself that the problem wasn't me, ensuring that any rejection wouldn't feel like my fault. I finally heard this realization loud and clear, and for the first time, I was able to disagree with it: *Of course, it wasn't my fault.* But just because we understand something mentally does not ensure change. We need to do the deep work of the somatic release to integrate the inner child. I had done so much of that work, but now I was being asked to put it into consistent, daily action.

In my relationship and friendships, I now had a reflection that was positive and beautiful. I was no longer in an environment that judged me in any way. No one was scapegoating me. I had literally escaped that role by changing how I interacted with myself. I began to relax and let my body tell me what it needed, rather than trying to control it all the time.

Soon after this, I was diagnosed with Hashimoto's disease. This autoimmune disease causes the body's thyroid gland to attack itself. I found it significant that this condition affected my throat, which was related to expressing my truth. I viewed this as a block to my own truth for so many years, which was now safe enough to reveal itself.

I realized that I'd had to shut down my intuition and go against myself to feel safe for so long, and my body was mirroring that. That was now changing, but it took time to break the cycle of momentum. The symptoms were emerging as signals that needed my attention.

When dealing with an autoimmune disease or any illness, it's crucial to truly tune in to your body to heal. I knew that something might come up now that my system was at rest. I began to truly listen to what my body wanted to eat, rather than relying on what I thought I should eat. I stopped working out almost entirely.

At first, I worried about gaining weight, an old fear of mine. What was so ridiculous about this was that I was always naturally very fit and thin. So, again, these fears were never based in reality. But this is another common theme I hear in my work: We don't feel safe owning what we are out of fear that it will leave. We never feel safe giving ourselves compliments or admiring ourselves too much. I had created a false image of myself in my head, so I always felt not enough and always pushed myself just in case.

However, within just a couple of months, I looked and felt better than ever. My intense workouts had been putting too much stress on my system and causing me to hold on to water weight due to cortisol. This started to leave quickly, and I started to feel lighter, leaner, and more at peace.

My mind became clearer, and I began to feel comfortable with this new sense of ease. I focused on fulfilling my actual needs rather than adhering to my idealized expectations. Instead of engaging in strenuous workouts, I began to take walks, listening to podcasts or inspiring YouTube videos while I did my special daily hike with my dog.

I reconnected with my body in a way I had never experienced before. I was living out the "ideal versus real" phase. While I didn't enjoy taking medication for my thyroid, I understood it was necessary for my healing process. I started to cultivate trust in my body's natural state, and this brought me genuine happiness. Within a year, I achieved remission, and my autoimmune symptoms became nonexistent.

I discovered a lifestyle that helped me maintain my balance, which was entirely new to me. It has been over a decade since my diagnosis, and I have remained in remission. I haven't experienced significant autoimmune flare-ups in many years, but early on, I realized that adjustments were necessary.

The most crucial adjustment was related to stress. I asked myself: *What am I stressed about? How am I contributing to my own stress?* It became my job to be kind to myself.

My new priority became creating an environment where my body felt safe and relaxed, rather than stressed and constantly on edge. Embracing this new environment brought up many reflections about my childhood. As we heal, we will always be asked to revisit things to reframe any lingering stress.

I reflected on how, in the past, I was always worried that I was doing something wrong. I would exhaust myself every day, trying my best yet still feel scapegoated when something went awry. It felt like I could never win, and my body was now just done with that relentless struggle.

From my childhood to my toxic relationships, I saw the same effect: one day I would be feeling loved, and the next I would be abandoned. The inconsistency keeps our nervous system in dysregulation. Ultimately, the body will break down when survival mode becomes a default setting for the nervous system. We cannot heal, find healthy love, or make an abundant income in such a state. A regulated nervous system is the only way to operate at our highest potential.

Love & Money

As I delved deeper into my new insights, I saw a profound connection between money and relationships. They are the same frequency. As my nervous system learned to relax, I also began bringing in more money than I had ever seen. Survival mode has everything to do with the lack of abundance you are feeling within. It's a catch-22 because not having love or money is what puts you in survival mode, but trust is what will pull you out. The more unapologetically I was connected to what was true for me, the more opportunities found me.

Many clients come to me for business mentorship to help them build their brand just as I have. The first thing I do with them is look into their emotional blocks. We cannot open the channel for abundance until we are fully open to our truth. My journey with building personal wealth started when I stopped outsourcing my power to others.

Webster's Dictionary defines "codependency" as excessive emotional or psychological reliance on a partner, typically one who requires support due to illness or addiction. A hallmark of codependency is an unhealthy sense of responsibility for others, paired with an over-reliance on them. Picture a parent you depend on who is also dependent on alcohol or addicted to love, emotional chaos, or perfection. This is depending on undependable people.

Sensitive souls are particularly vulnerable to what I call "vibrational codependency." When you deeply empathize with others' emotions, it becomes easy to absorb and carry emotional burdens that aren't yours.

Many sensitive people grow up feeling blamed, judged, and misunderstood, leading them to believe that they are at fault for problems around them. But there is also a toxic empathy. This is when you feel bad for the one who is hurting you. This is another version of over-responsibility that creates energetic codependency. When too much of your energy is given away without boundaries, it takes a toll on you.

As sensitive souls enter romantic relationships, it's crucial to observe the behaviors of both partners carefully. All codependent relationships involve two partners exhibiting codependent behaviors.

Whether one partner leans towards narcissism or extreme self-absorption or not, the core dynamic remains the same: a false belief that survival depends on the other person. The narcissist is dependent on the codependent as a supply. The codependent is dependent on the narcissist's affection. To gain a narcissist's affection, the codependent will over-please and fix and, in turn, abandon their standards.

Many unhealed empaths wrestle with the inner message that they cannot fully thrive on their own. This capability issue is front and center. This belief is rooted in negative self-judgment that is both untrue and harmful.

Due to their intense emotional experiences and deep sensitivity, sensitive souls may struggle with love addiction and clinginess, arising from a desperate need to feel whole through another person. Because they often feel like outsiders and different from those around them, when they find a connection, it can become unhealthy if old wounds and misinterpretations remain unhealed.

For years, I had no idea I was addicted to love. I recognized that I chose partners who struggled with addiction or exhibited narcissistic traits, but I never connected the dots. I was only able to do so and break free when I started trusting myself and prioritizing my needs. But the deeper layer was when I became fully available to the parts I feared within.

When you believe there's something wrong with you, you may avoid deep intimacy with another person. On one hand, you want them to validate your worth. On the other hand, you fear that they won't. This is a struggle, and it is also how we outsource our power.

This is how so many people remain trapped in toxic cycles, giving others permission to validate their self-worth or sense of safety.

Lisa

Lisa, a client of mine for a couple of years, grew up in a toxic home. However, when we first started working together, she wasn't fully aware of the extent of that toxicity.

It took her a year to realize that her mother was the main issue in her life. I frequently say, "Mother equals other." Based on the relationship patterns she presented, it was clear that her original wound, her attachment injury, stemmed from her relationship with her mother.

Like many clients, when Lisa first found me, she resonated with what I was saying but wasn't yet clear on her deeper issue. Lisa had done a ton of inner work, but she still hadn't found the missing piece. She was in a relationship with a difficult partner, and while she related to my social media content, she wasn't sure if he truly had avoidant traits or if she was the problem.

Lisa came to the realization that her mother had been jealous of her. Lisa recognized that whenever she wanted something, her mother would disagree or discourage her. Striving for success and physical perfection, Lisa tried relentlessly to make every aspect of her life perfect, hoping her mother would finally acknowledge her.

Lisa felt as if she were programmed to earn love. I helped her understand that the reason her mother scapegoated her wasn't due to a failure to recognize Lisa's goodness, but because her mother couldn't bear to let Lisa see her own value.

Her mother's only way of exerting control was to make Lisa doubt herself, which allowed her to avoid feeling inadequate in comparison. This dynamic is common and can be incredibly confusing; many might wonder how a mother could be jealous of her own daughter.

It helps to think of it this way: it's a reflection of generational trauma. Her mother never had the chance to realize her dreams, and seeing her daughter pursue her own was triggering. A healthy mother would love to give her daughter everything she herself didn't get, but a wounded mother can become threatened when she sees her daughter get opportunities that were denied to her. "Hurt people hurt people," and yes, even their own daughters.

In her avoidant relationship, Lisa placed her partner on a pedestal and overlooked the red flags. He was the first man she'd dated who possessed wealth, prestige, a supportive family, and numerous friends, qualities that made him represent worthiness in her eyes.

His interest in her made her feel valued, as if being chosen by such a remarkable person validated her self-worth. He also mirrored some of the aspects of her identity that her mother had never acknowledged. This led Lisa to become increasingly reliant on him for that external validation.

As the months passed in their relationship, her insecurities grew as his commitment waned. She was in the typical avoidant cycle. He love-bombed her, then started to fear the closeness and pulled back emotionally. He would nitpick and criticize her in small ways. Then he would make those things the reason for his pulling back. Lisa was beginning to wonder why she couldn't do anything right.

I reminded her that she was doing everything right, but he needed to find an issue with it anyway so that he had an excuse to pull away. He would then ghost her for a few days, sometimes a week, and then start breadcrumbing her with little text messages or acts of service. An avoidant person has one love language, and that is acts of service. Acts of service don't require emotional connection.

We worked on helping her establish her self-worth independently of him. I gave her some inner, outer, and energetic boundaries to practice. The first step was building up Lisa's emotional autonomy. She began to understand why she had idealized him and recognized him as a false source of validation. It became clear to her that he embodied the traits society deemed worthy: flashy titles and a social circle that she lacked.

In her eyes, he seemed superior, representing everything she believed she needed to be to gain her mother's approval. I encouraged her to examine the situation more deeply.

This man had all the outward appearances of success, but internally, he treated her poorly when she did not cater to him. A man who understands his worth does not behave this way. I pointed out to her that he was using coercive control and intermittent reinforcement to keep her hooked and maintain his power over her.

This dynamic often creates love addiction or trauma bonds. Their relationship was characterized by a traumatic bond. She recognized that his struggle with his own self-worth had led him to create such a perfect exterior.

The key lesson here is that external success does not heal internal wounds. Lisa and her partner both depended on external validation to affirm their worth, but this approach was not working. True self-worth comes from knowing your value, regardless of image or status. They were relying on each other, but neither was stable.

Lisa experienced some withdrawal symptoms, but we were able to work through them with some serious dedication. In a few months, she decided to move on, and though it was hard, the light came back into her eyes, and she felt solid.

After our work together, Lisa felt transformed. I could see that she had reclaimed her energy and was no longer willing to outsource her power to her partner, who had appeared so dominant. She was beginning to recognize the red flags for what they truly were, rather than avoiding them. Instead of focusing on appearances or status, she started to pay attention to her feelings.

Breaking free from patterns of love addiction and trauma bonds involves ending reliance on external power and reconnecting with oneself. The process is intense; you may experience withdrawal and self-doubt. Obsessive thoughts may arise; these are all symptoms of weaning yourself off the "drug" of love.

Upper Limit Issues

Often, when we are disconnected from our own abundance, we fall into an upper limit issue. I first encountered this term while reading *Conscious Loving* by Gay Hendricks and Katherine Hendricks. While the term was new to me, the experience was familiar.

The "upper limits problem" refers to the tendency to unconsciously sabotage positive growth in our lives. This can happen in areas such as new relationships, career success, or overcoming addiction. Just when things start to improve, we create conflict or chaos to restore balance. This occurs because we have internalized a false belief that happiness and success must be tempered with pain; we feel unworthy of sustained joy.

Personally, my upper limits problem often manifested in relationships and careers, as those were my primary sources of validation. The moment I fell deeply in love, a wave of discomfort would arise.

I often found myself confused, wondering whether my relationship was flawed or if I was being punished for something. I would instigate fights or abruptly break up for no apparent reason, only to feel relief afterward, as if pushing love away was a safe escape from vulnerability. For years, it felt like a dark force was sabotaging every perfect moment.

It's strange to strive for perfection, then find yourself unable to handle it when it arrives. I felt victimized, as if something outside of me was punishing my happiness. This despair led me to ask deeper questions about spiritual laws and to ponder what I might be missing. How did life work? Was this something in me or outside of me? Were the things I was experiencing based on my perception or based on reality? This was when I began to understand that how we relate to the issue is the issue. I related to experiences through a lens of trauma.

My studies quickly led to a breakthrough when I learned about patterns and how they are created and sustained by our beliefs and judgments. I discovered that I could heal from the inside out, and so could others.

Due to conditioning, sensitive souls often wrestle with issues of upper limits. The fear of greatness or success can be paralyzing. The good news is that once you recognize these belief patterns and get to the original time it started, they lose their power. But until then, we can stay in a pattern of sabotaging our own efforts for more.

I would also sabotage my career. I remember the night before a huge cover shoot for *Runner's World* magazine. In a moment of impulsivity, I decided to eat an entire pan of brownies. I couldn't stop the urge. This way, if the photographers said I didn't look good, I would know it was because of something I did, something I could control.

This gave me a sense of ease. If they rejected me without explanation, I would spiral into thinking I was damaged again. Sabotaging myself insulated me from the pain and shock of rejection.

However, I recall that photo shoot as one of my best. My attempt at sabotage didn't work. The more that happened, the less I wanted to sabotage myself. My old patterns were losing power.

It became a safer space for me to trust myself, to desire something, and have it reflected back to me. That was a new experience. I needed to practice this pattern over time to re-regulate my nervous system.

Awareness is the first step, but the next is realizing that you hold the tools for change. Anything blocking your flow of joy signals the need for action. I transformed my upper limits issue by consciously choosing love over fear, time and time again.

I talked myself through my fears and patterns, committing to courage over avoidance and reclaiming my power moment by moment. This is the essence of self-healing: finding your own answers through honest self-inquiry rather than relying on external validation.

Exercise: One of my favorite activities with clients is creating a safe space. To do this, close your eyes and breathe in through the nose and out through the mouth.

Now, examine the fear that you are facing. Look closely at the fear of achieving everything you desire. Pay attention to what this fear is telling you.

Give it a voice: *If I acquire the love of my life, then what?* Often, the answer is that this love might leave, confirming your initial belief that you are unworthy or broken.

Sometimes, the fear stems from the uncertainty of what it would look or feel like to have what you want. The unknown can be even more frightening, as it opens the door to the possibility of failure. So, let's return to the question with eyes closed:

What if I got everything I wanted? Notice what feelings arise. Acknowledge if you find yourself unsure, as that can be frightening.

Identify if this uncertainty evolves into a significant fear. Pay attention to where you feel it in your body. Then ask yourself: *Do I believe it's possible to have everything I want? Is it even a possibility for me? Do I need to expand my window of tolerance and enhance my capacity to allow this in*? This is your capacity training. *Can I expand my capacity to hold fear at the same time as I continue to walk towards the thing I desire?*

Next, consider whether you are okay with not knowing what it would look like or feel like, or even whether it's attainable. Notice the emotions that come to the surface. Hold space for these feelings instead of always trying to protect yourself from them. Look at them and also notice that your body is still safe.

Ask yourself: *Do I feel capable of holding on to my dreams, or am I afraid I will fail and ruin them?* This reflects an old pattern of self-sabotage. Acknowledge what arises. Ask yourself if you are, in fact, capable of exploring your dreams and allowing yourself to make mistakes. When you fear your dreams, it is because you don't know if you can do it right. Give yourself the option to make mistakes and to keep trying anyway. That sentence alone will give you permission to move forward without having to be perfect. This will take the pressure off.

The key is to accept all of this and still embrace your true self as perfection in the process.

Continue This Experience by Trying This: Visualize your dream. Simultaneously, recognize any fear or negative emotions that surface. Allow both to coexist as you engage in this process.

Keep your vision of the dream clear while acknowledging the old, uncomfortable feelings that are present as well. Now imagine someone alongside you in this space, perhaps me, a therapist, a coach, or a comforting figure like an imaginary fairy godmother.

I once used the "fairy godmother" analogy because I lacked support at the time. We need to create the energy of the person we wish we had if we don't actually have someone in our lives who feels supportive. This is also how we begin to rely on a higher power.

Observe the scenario unfold. Once you've noticed the uncomfortable feelings, bring your focus back to your dream.

Picture yourself moving closer to this dream. As you do, let your feelings intensify, but don't let them overwhelm you. Continue to recognize these negative feelings while diving deeper into the vivid details of your ideal life.

This will be a journey, but you are training your capacity to manage both the positive and the negative. As you learn to tolerate the negative emotions without allowing them to gain power, you will enhance your ability to embrace even more positivity.

This is shadow work. If we don't allow ourselves to integrate the negative aspects of our lives, we can't fully embrace the positive. We need to learn to hold space for all occurrences in life and become the dominant energy for what we wish to create.

Practice this daily, and over time, you'll notice that negative feelings lose their power and your dreams become more attainable. Many healing paradigms ask a dangerous question: *What's wrong with you?* However, for those breaking the cycle, the real question is: *Where did you abandon yourself to survive?*

When a sensitive soul is told they're too much, too sensitive, too emotional, or too difficult, they internalize that belief, making it part of their nature. They begin to think their true self is the problem, leading them to try to fix, shrink, control, or discipline themselves into acceptance.

We abandon part of our emotional truth and the understanding that "how we do one thing, we do all things." So, if you abandon the negative emotions, you are also abandoning the golden shadow, which is your shine. When we are abandoning parts of our emotional truth, we are not working with our full abundance.

The golden shadow is the most powerful part of us, one that we fear the most. Yes, we fear that we are not enough, but the bigger fear is that we are more than enough. When we know our potential and then look back at the years we denied it because someone else made us doubt it, we feel upset and confused. So, we bury these feelings until we are ready to truly own them.

However, the more you hide your perceived flaws, the more your shine gets dimmed. The mindset of partial self-abandonment can lead to deeper illness. Healing does not come from correcting who you are. It comes from easing the internal conflict with yourself. Illness can serve as a wake-up call rather than a punishment.

There comes a moment, sometimes devastating, when the body forces a reckoning, a diagnosis, a breakdown, or an inability to function as before. This moment is not the body's betrayal; it is an intervention. The body is saying, *I will no longer carry what you refuse to confront.*

For many cycle breakers, illness becomes the first boundary they were never allowed to set.

Kelly

Kelly has been my client for five years. When she first came to me, she was sixty years old.

She had been in a marriage for thirty years, spending most of that time bedridden. Kelly was desperate to reclaim her life and was tired of feeling fully responsible for her illness.

She grew up with a mother who had borderline personality disorder and an angry father. Despite excelling in school and being a high achiever, Kelly never received credit for her accomplishments. She became the family scapegoat. While she recognized her mother's issues, she could not escape the constant blame her mother placed on her.

Although Kelly loved her mother, she never felt loved in return by either parent. Her father often told her that her achievements weren't enough and withheld affection. Her mother acknowledged her success but never attended her games or recitals. Kelly felt invisible and profoundly invalidated. Although her story is similar to Lisa's, it has its differences.

Feeling helpless in her quest for validation, Kelly believed that if she could gain love from someone considered worthy, maybe her mother would see it, too. As a result, she married a doctor who came from a seemingly perfect family. He was intelligent and educated, and they shared moral values and religious practices. They had four children and appeared to lead a happy life. However, shortly after marrying, Kelly began to feel scapegoated by her husband and his family, often without realizing it.

Kelly found it difficult to express her points of view. When she spoke up and disagreed, she quickly realized that opposing his family's opinions meant being sidelined. Once again, she felt invalidated. She struggled to be recognized as talented or intelligent. In conversations, when she expressed differing opinions, they would ostracize her.

As a result, Kelly sank into chronic fatigue. The man she believed she'd married, along with the family she'd thought would support her, ended up bringing her back to her old wounds.

I shared my belief with her that her chronic fatigue was her body's way of seeking an escape from the conflict. I also understood that her body was reflecting her struggle to own her identity as a "problem."

Our bodies often mirror our habitual beliefs, and breaking that cycle takes time. Kelly became the one who was sick, bedridden, and unable to travel with her husband or attend family gatherings. While this condition allowed her to avoid confrontation, it also placed her back in the role of the problem. As her husband enjoyed a vibrant life, she suffered in silence, isolated and filled with shame. Exhausted by this cycle, her body ultimately forced her to retreat.

At one point, Kelly even visited a mental institution because she felt overwhelmed by her internal turmoil, with nowhere to direct her emotions. But she wasn't mentally ill; she was simply breaking down. Her life mirrored her childhood, but with a veneer of higher status.

Now part of a family of doctors, she still felt left out.

What she desired from her family always seemed just out of reach.

Her inner child had learned that the safest place to be was in the role of the problem. Over the subsequent years, I empowered

Kelly to recognize that her feelings were valid, even in a system that required her to be wrong. She realized she had married into a family with narcissistic tendencies. She also realized that she had signed up for this on some level. This was Kelly's opportunity to rewrite history.

The family members were superficial and only supported a certain narrative. Anyone who threatened their perfect image had to be labeled as the problem because admitting to any wrongdoing was unthinkable for them. Once again, Kelly felt helpless, and despair began to set in.

The more we empowered her to recognize that her perspective was valid, the more she realized she was facing systems in her life that were contrary to her views. We not only started to validate her feelings, but we also acknowledged the opposing viewpoints of others, even though those perspectives seemed quite one-sided. She had to learn how to coexist in a reality that was not shared. No one's viewpoint needed to be wrong, but it did need to be acknowledged as wrong for her.

People who live authentically can validate others' opinions. In contrast, those who struggle to accept differing opinions often feel the need to negate them because they are insecure about the truth of their own beliefs. These people typically lack a strong sense of self-worth.

They often require control over a narrative to feel valued, which is another instance of relying on unreliable people. This behavior arises when we haven't fully learned to trust ourselves. So, instead of Kelly needing them to be wrong to validate that she was right, she needed to see that two realities can coexist, but they need to be open to each other. Kelly married into a family that was not allowing her differences of opinion, but not allowing their opinions was also hurting her. She needed to learn to expand her capacity to see that no one needed to be wrong for her to be right.

I introduced a new perspective to Kelly. I explained that we live in a narcissistic society that promotes a single standard of beauty, a singular way to learn, and so forth. Certain people gain higher status through greater achievements, but this does not necessarily equate to higher worth.

These achievements are rooted in a system that only values hierarchy. Once we broke this down and she could see herself more clearly, Kelly began to feel relief. A year after we started our work together, Kelly took her first flight in over thirty years.

She was no longer dealing with chronic fatigue. She even purchased a passport and took her first international trip, astonished that this was actually happening.

During this period, she would still experience occasional bouts of exhaustion, but she had learned how to reset herself. She began to advocate for herself, refusing to let the negative inner dialogue pull her back down.

Kelly started discussing her newfound truths with her husband. Although he was initially resistant, he began to show her some respect because her arguments made sense. She recognized his discomfort when she rejected the role of the problem in their relationship. However, she no longer agreed with his rejection of her, and this gave her strength. In real time, she saw that he relied on her to stay in that role to feel superior.

This realization extended to her family as well, prompting her to reflect on her upbringing. She understood that the role she played in her family was not her identity; rather, it was a place she needed to occupy for the family's dysfunction to continue. This was when Kelly started rewriting history and finding herself in a new identity. She was not the problem child; she was the one who expressed the systemic problem.

Now, at sixty-five, Kelly is well on her way to becoming the most powerful voice in her family, a voice of reason, truth, and leadership. Her role is evolving, and she is focused on embodying the alignment she has so gratefully discovered.

She's working on her first book, which focuses on this journey. When she came to me five years ago, she believed I was her last hope. I encouraged her to stick with me, assuring her that one day she would be living the life she was meant to lead.

I told her I envisioned her on stages and writing books, but she didn't believe me. However, here's the truth:

It's never too late to pursue your soul's purpose. As we heal, our lives begin to align with who we truly are. It's about going against the system, not against ourselves.

Here's the reframe that changes everything: you didn't become sick because you were weak; you became sick because you were strong enough to endure in the wrong environment for too long.

Healing begins when you shift your perspective on resistance. Rather than fighting against your body, you challenge the way you relate to the system. Instead of ignoring your intuition, you choose to honor it. Instead of bending yourself to fit in, you choose alignment, even if it costs you relationships, roles, or identities. This is where true recovery starts.

Healing is not about instant relief; it's about reorientation. It involves leaving environments that require self-betrayal, ending relationships that thrive on your silence, and choosing to eat, rest, and move in ways that nurture your nervous system. It means saying no without feeling the need to explain yourself and allowing your body to recalibrate away from constant threat.

As you find more alignment, your symptoms often start to ease, not because you've fixed yourself, but because the inner conflict has ended. The body can relax when the soul is no longer under siege.

Chapter Summary

- **Spiritual Dis-ease as Self-Betrayal:** The chapter introduces "spiritual dis-ease" as the body's response to prolonged misalignment with one's truth. Symptoms like anxiety, fatigue, depression, and illness are reframed not as failures but as signals that the individual has been suppressing their authentic self for too long.
- **The Body as Messenger, Not Enemy:** Physical and emotional symptoms are presented as intelligent adaptations to chronic stress, trauma, and self-abandonment. Whether through eating disorders, autoimmune conditions, or anxiety, the body expresses what the voice has been unable to communicate, revealing the cost of living out of alignment.
- **Perfectionism, Control, and Coping Mechanisms:** The author explains how perfectionism and control-based behaviors develop as survival strategies to avoid rejection and create a sense of safety. However, these patterns ultimately reinforce self-abandonment and deepen internal conflict rather than resolve it.
- **Healing Through Alignment and Nervous System Safety:** True healing begins when individuals stop

overriding their needs and start listening to their bodies. By shifting from "shoulds" to authentic desires, reducing stress, and creating safe internal and external environments, the nervous system can regulate, allowing the body to move toward balance and even remission.

- **Codependency, Love Addiction, and Energy Misplacement:** The chapter explores how sensitive individuals often become codependent, seeking validation and safety through others while overgiving and absorbing emotional burdens. Breaking these patterns requires reclaiming personal power, setting boundaries, and becoming the primary source of one's own safety and worth.
- **Upper Limits and Self-Sabotage:** Many cycle breakers unconsciously sabotage success, love, or happiness due to deeply ingrained beliefs about unworthiness. Recognizing and expanding one's capacity to hold both fear and desire allows individuals to move beyond these limits and sustain growth without collapse.
- **Illness as a Turning Point for Awakening:** Through client stories like Kelly's, the chapter illustrates how chronic illness can act as a forced boundary and a catalyst for transformation. Healing occurs not by "fixing" oneself, but by ending self-abandonment, validating one's truth, and choosing alignment over conformity.
- **Reclaiming Truth and Embodying Healing:** The core message is that illness is not punishment but intervention. When sensitive souls stop betraying themselves and begin living in alignment with their truth, the body can finally relax, and symptoms often ease. Healing is a process of reorientation—choosing authenticity, self-trust, and inner coherence over external approval.

PART 3

THE INTEGRATION

CHAPTER 7

SYSTEM UPGRADE

Get real about how you feel so you can heal.

What happens when you stop merely understanding and start truly embodying?

This is a phase of awakening that no one prepares you for. The soul who is the sensitive one, often the scapegoat and the cycle breaker, is also the one who is here to upgrade their system. In doing so, they elevate the consciousness of the world.

The phase of your awakening comes after gaining insight, completing therapy, recognizing patterns, and doing inner-child work. It arrives after you finally understand why your life unfolded the way it did. This phase is embodiment, and it changes everything.

When my system began to upgrade, my life also urged me to step into a new role. Much of this involved ego death and evolving into my true self. The divorce was significant for me, and I knew my soul was prompting me to embrace my calling in a more visible way. I was being asked to exemplify my work as it grew deeper.

You can intellectually understand your trauma and still live within its confines. You can speak the language of healing and continue to organize your life around old survival strategies. Embodiment happens when the nervous system updates, not just the mind.

This is what I refer to as a "system upgrade." Your body begins to reject what your mind once accepted. What once felt normal starts to feel unbearable: emotional inconsistency, subtle manipulation, self-betrayal disguised as compassion, and environments that dull your clarity.

You're no longer willing to live misaligned, even quietly. As embodiment deepens, familiar strategies cease to work. Over-functioning leads to exhaustion. People-pleasing triggers resentment. Explaining yourself becomes draining. Remaining silent feels like a weight on your system.

This is not regression; it is integration. Your system reorganizes itself around truth instead of safety.

Matt

Matt was married when he came to me. He was a successful neurosurgeon and had a beautiful wife and two adorable dogs. His life looked perfect. In fact, when we first met, he said, "Candace, there's something wrong with me. My life is literally perfect, yet I have been struggling with this chronic illness for years. What am I doing wrong?"

Like many people, Matt believed that living a picture-perfect life, having wealth, a spouse, and a prestigious career, was the solution to all his problems. However, this often highlights the deeper issues that lie beneath the beautiful façade.

Matt truly loved his wife and was proud of his accomplishments. However, he was deeply unhappy in a marriage with an emotionally avoidant partner. He had chosen this type of partner because emotional intimacy would have required him to confront wounds he was still avoiding.

At the time of his marriage, ten years earlier, Matt preferred this arrangement. Being married to someone who was emotionally attuned would have forced him to face his own emotional wounds, which he was not ready to do. He felt he needed to avoid confronting his emotional truth in order to maintain the high-level image of his life.

He shared with me that as a child, he often felt like the odd one out. He was shorter, small, and not particularly attractive, but smart. No girls ever paid him any attention, and he never went on any dates. This made him feel powerless and invisible. Additionally, his family was dysfunctional. For many years, he lied to himself about this situation, but now he could no longer deny the truth.

He acknowledged that he had a controlling mother and a father who always went along with her. He wasn't allowed to explore himself or be anything his mother did not approve of, which left him oscillating between the roles of the golden child and the scapegoat.

Given that his mother had low self-esteem, she lavished attention on anyone who was particularly successful or conformed to societal ideals of being elite. Early on, Matt decided he would become the ideal son to earn his mother's consistent approval. He concluded that success would be his currency for love.

Thus, he became a doctor, married another doctor, and built an ostensibly perfect life. He didn't choose medicine because it inspired him; he chose it because it was a path that garnered societal rewards.

His mother praised him for his accomplishments, and while he still never felt truly listened to or cared for, that praise was enough for him at the time. As he began to realize that his so-called perfect life was not fulfilling the emotional needs he lacked in childhood, he sought my help.

My first question to Matt was, "Do you love your wife?"

I asked him about the kinds of things they talked about and what their dreams together were. He mentioned they both wanted children, but after being married for over ten years, those children were still not a reality. Did they both desire the image of a family without genuinely wanting the family unit itself? He acknowledged that they functioned well as business partners, but he longed for a deeper emotional connection, which he felt she could not provide.

I then asked him if he believed he could create that emotional connection. Matt's deepest fear was loneliness. I told him that there is always a transitional period when we shift from living in our heads to embracing our feelings more fully.

It takes time to integrate and deeply connect with our inner child, which helps us feel less alone. Many of us fear this deep connection to our inner child because we fear we will have to give up the things that brought us validation. So we start to fear the inner child or stay distant from it as if it is the problem. When we learn that it is safe to exist without needing to perform, that's when our lives begin to align naturally.

During this integration period, people may enter our lives who don't resonate with us. It's important to use our discernment to say no and wait for the right connections to come along. This can be a scary time because the fear of loneliness and not belonging will be front and center. But this is also the phase in which we learn to connect deeply with our own needs and desires, regardless of whether they are shared. We start to become creators of our own reality, rather than allowing external circumstances to dictate our friendships, careers, or identities.

Matt and I engaged in months of deep inner-child work. He rediscovered that he had always been a highly sensitive child but felt compelled to suppress that sensitivity because he didn't think it was manly. Additionally, he revealed that he pursued a career as a doctor primarily for the status, despite feeling disillusioned with the healthcare system. While he enjoyed helping people, he found the workplace politics increasingly intolerable.

Matt's childhood dream had always been to be a writer, so I encouraged him to start writing. One of Matt's chronic illnesses was a sleep disorder. He could not sleep much, let alone dream. But as he began this process with me, he began to dream again, and he experienced dreams that brought back forgotten or buried memories from his childhood.

I introduced him to a technique called "melting memories," which we can start to practice when we begin to feel safe in our bodies. In this state, as cortisol levels decrease in the brain, memories begin to resurface.

Matt had also undergone multiple surgeries to address his sleep issues in the previous years, but nothing had quite worked for him. After we started our work together and he began to connect with his inner child, his sleep patterns fluctuated between improvement and relapse. He was learning to regulate his nervous system in new ways.

Although he was grappling with his true self, he was also interested in the possible new direction his life was taking. Sensitive minds can often feel stifled within rigid systems, not out of weakness, but because they perceive possibilities beyond those constraints. Eventually, Matt realized new possibilities and could no longer continue practicing as a doctor; it no longer aligned with his authentic self.

He aspired to become a holistic practitioner, so he returned to training. During this transformative period, he also went through a divorce and moved to another state, distancing himself from his toxic family. However, this initially led to a bit of a downward spiral; he wasn't fully embodied yet.

Although Matt was taking aligned actions, he still held on to past emotions. He had done half of the work by making bold moves, but he recognized that he wasn't doing the emotional work; he was bypassing it. It's essential for the body to mourn the old paradigm before it can fully trust in the new one.

At first, Matt thought he was doing something wrong, but I reassured him that wasn't the case; he had just been leaving out a critical step in the process. He admitted he hadn't done the emotional homework I had given him because he thought he could just move through the actions without going through the emotions.

You can't change your life without also addressing your emotions. Even though we had been doing inner-child work, Matt wasn't fully applying what he had learned. You would think that, with all these positive changes, he would be thriving, but it's essential to also walk through the emotional processes to truly embody them.

If you don't give yourselves the space to do this emotional work, you risk facing a narrative that your inner child has been trying to avoid for years. The inner child is most afraid of you abandoning them, and that means abandoning what you feel. The fear is real, and you need to allow time for everything to settle.

People often want healing to happen quickly, but if they skip the proper steps, they'll find themselves falling back into old patterns. So, I provided Matt with some emotional release practices and encouraged him to visualize his desired life. This is a key point:

You must feel the reality you want before it can anchor in your body. You can live this new life, but you won't feel it. Again, you risk feeling like an imposter or disconnected from the things you have worked so hard to enjoy. Embodiment comes before evidence. When things don't align immediately, it's not a sign of failure; it's a recalibration.

After I assigned this homework, Matt said he had started meditating for up to thirty minutes every day. He described a profound experience when he envisioned the woman of his dreams walking through the door. He felt fear but also excitement. Matt trained himself to continue allowing the visions, along with the fears. Over time, he was able to go deep into his imagination; he even pictured the meals they would cook together. He felt that they were aligned in purpose and lifestyle. Although he wasn't sure if this would truly happen, as long as he could feel it as real, he maintained faith that one day she would enter his life. Matt understood the assignment.

A few months later, Matt called me. "Candace, you were right! I met her, and she's conscious. We walk on the beach together, discussing our inner-child work. She appreciates my sensitivity and awareness, and guess what? She's a coach who teaches this stuff!" He shared with her that he was exploring a vegan diet, and it turned out she was a vegan, too.

Matt's life took some time to align because, for forty-five years, he had been living in a different frequency. It wasn't safe for him to step into the new reality just yet. The upgrade to Matt's system was all about allowing his feeling dimension to lead rather than his actions alone.

When changes don't happen right away, it's not because we are doing something wrong or not being spiritual enough. It's because our body and system need to trust this new way. Our body and mind must practice this new emotional reality before it can actually show up in our lives.

Get Real About How You Feel so You Can Heal

Many people make the mistake of needing to see reality to initiate their feelings. This is a codependent approach. The embodied way is to embody the frequency you wish to attract.

When we are consistent and dedicated to the path of integration, our lives will transform. The main barrier to accessing higher frequencies is the emotional wounds we still carry, which serve as debris and create resistance. Through regular practice of inner-child work, we can integrate these experiences, allowing a higher frequency to become our new state of being.

Before I guided Matt through his transformation, I was navigating my own self-upgrade journey. For years, I lived a life that many would admire, modeling and acting on stages, performing roles scripted by the expectations of others.

However, beneath the glamour and applause, I felt a deep disconnection from my true self, a persistent whisper that I was meant for something far more authentic and powerful. The external roles I played became intolerable internally. Since childhood, I had been searching for a deeper path but found no real home within society's confines.

I struggled for years, trying to navigate a career that I thought was alternative yet was still governed by a rigid narrative. Silently, I was screaming for my true path to reveal itself. As I grew unapologetic in claiming this desire and engaged in inner work to discover my authority, my path finally unfolded.

The internal dissonance became impossible to ignore. I stepped away from the world and immersed myself in spiritual psychology, a rigorous, often painful, yet ultimately liberating journey of healing and embodiment. It was in this space that I found the true stage of my life.

On this stage, I embraced my genuine purpose, becoming not only a healed person but also a leader, a guide, and a coach who holds space for others to break free from old systems and step fully into their sovereignty. My journey revealed a critical truth: no matter how polished or perfect our external lives may seem, lasting transformation occurs only when our nervous system aligns with our soul's truth.

When you begin to live unapologetically from that place, embodiment becomes the true system upgrade, the foundation from which all authentic change flows. This transformation cannot fully take form until you release the false idols of acceptance, external validation, and the need to prove yourself.

Upon achieving this embodiment, you move from mere survival to true sovereignty.

Why do relationships often shift or end during this period? When you embody your truth, you stop managing others' emotions. You can no longer be in partnership with people who need you to be different from who you authentically are. You no longer put people on a pedestal because you now bow to your inner child.

This alone can destabilize many dynamics. People who relied on your empathy without reciprocation, your flexibility without accountability, and your silence to maintain comfort may perceive your embodiment as rejection. It isn't; it's reorganization. Your system is no longer available to carry what others refuse to hold. There is no more room for negotiation.

Before embodiment, you focus on alignment. After embodiment, misalignment manifests as physical distress. Your body becomes the authority.

This is the upgrade: you no longer need permission.

One of the clearest signs that a system is outdated is when it begins labeling visionaries as "disordered." The dramatic rise in ADHD and neurodivergent diagnoses is not happening because something has suddenly gone wrong with humanity. It's happening because more people are being born with nervous systems that no longer align with linear productivity, emotional suppression, or hierarchical control.

These traits are not deficits; they represent incompatibilities with a system that was never designed for truth, intuition, or multidimensional perception. Highly sensitive, neurodivergent people do not lack focus; they possess nonlinear intelligence.

Their awareness navigates through emotion, patterns, meanings, and possibilities simultaneously. This type of mind does not thrive in rigid environments that reward obedience over originality and compliance over consciousness.

The system does not recognize differences; it sees them as wrong. Thus, it labels, manages, and medicates what it cannot control.

Remarkably, those who struggle the most within traditional roles often flourish once they leave those structures. Many highly sensitive neurodivergent adults feel chronically lost in conventional careers, not because they lack purpose, but because their current purpose was never meant to be assigned to them. Their work is not to fit into a pre-existing structure but to create a new one.

As their sense of embodiment deepens, many experience a sudden intolerance for workplaces that demand self-betrayal, emotional suppression, or submission to misaligned authority. What once felt stable can now feel suffocating. This is not avoidance or immaturity; it's a nervous system refusing to contort itself any longer.

For many people I work with, clarity does not come from trying harder within a system; it comes from stepping outside of it entirely. This is what a system upgrade looks like in real life. You stop asking, *What should I do*? and start asking, *What am I here to build?*

Highly sensitive and neurodivergent people are not here to optimize for efficiency. They are here to re-pattern reality through healing, leadership, creativity, innovation, education, and entirely new ways of relating to power, success, and service.

Your connection to your inner world is your source. Once you understand this, lifelong restlessness makes sense.

The boredom, the rebellion, and the refusal to settle are not signs of failure; they are indications that you are outgrowing the system.

Chapter Summary

- **Embodiment as the Real Upgrade:** The chapter explains that healing is incomplete until insight becomes embodiment. True transformation happens not just when the mind understands trauma, but when the nervous system reorganizes around truth instead of survival, making old patterns and misaligned environments feel intolerable.
- **Your Body Becomes the Authority:** As embodiment deepens, the body begins rejecting what the mind once tolerated, including people-pleasing, emotional inconsistency, subtle manipulation, and self-betrayal. This shift is framed not as regression, but as integration: the system is upgrading to live in alignment rather than mere safety.
- **Healing Requires Feeling, Not Just Action:** Through Matt's story, the chapter shows that making big external changes is not enough without emotional processing. Embodiment comes when a person allows grief, fear, and desire to be fully felt, teaching the body to trust the new reality before external evidence appears.
- **From External Success to Soul Alignment:** The chapter contrasts socially admired lives with deeply authentic ones, showing how prestige, status, and image can still leave a person emotionally empty. Real fulfillment

begins when people stop building their lives around validation and instead organize them around sensitivity, inner truth, and genuine purpose.

- **Relationships Reorganize Around Your Truth:** As people embody their authentic selves, many relationships shift or fall away because they are no longer willing to manage others' emotions or maintain roles built on self-abandonment. What looks like disruption is actually a reordering of life around sovereignty, reciprocity, and emotional honesty.
- **Neurodivergence and Sensitivity as Signs of a New Paradigm:** The chapter reframes ADHD and neurodivergence not as deficits, but as evidence that many people are no longer suited for rigid, linear, emotionally suppressive systems. Sensitive and nonlinear minds are presented as builders of new structures, here not to fit into outdated systems, but to create more conscious ways of living, working, and leading.

CHAPTER 8

YOUR HIGHER CALLING

Now that you are existing in your true role, you can call in your divine work. You were never meant to simply heal; you were meant to heal so that you could embody the work that will heal others and the world simply by being integrated.

Healing is not the destination; it is the preparation. Sensitive souls do not awaken just to feel better; they awaken to live differently. Your higher calling is not about saving others; it's about stepping away from systems that require your disconnection.

Your example is what will inspire others to join you. Many advanced souls are born into families in a world that feels wrong. For years, we have carried the question: *Why do I feel so deeply? Why does everyone else see things differently?* This leads us to believe there is something wrong with us, but we hold on to that doubt because those around us validate our feelings of wrongness.

In the last decade, while coaching others through deep emotional wound healing, I have seen that you are now ready to take your position as an embodied teacher and leader. Your transformation from Cinderella to Wonder Woman, from Peter

Pan to Superman, is significant. It is now your time to no longer be a symbol of the wounded but to embody the example of someone who is healed.

In this new consciousness, we no longer look up to people who merely talk; we look up to those who embody what they discuss. Many people who find me on YouTube say my descriptions resonate perfectly with them. People wonder how I could have described them so accurately. I always reply, "Because I was once you, and I had no one to guide me, so I followed the path less traveled and figured it out for myself. I don't only see you, I am you."

I healed myself and started to listen to the insights that came to me. My spiritual gifts were elevated in ways that bring me so much joy. I can channel the inner child for clients, I can connect dots that no one can see, and the reason I can do this is that I got out of my own way.

Embodiment is not about us personally; it is about healing so deeply that we clear the path for the divine to enter. The wisdom that drops in is a magical daily reality for me. My work is not about me; it is about being a vessel for God's work. We all share this purpose, but we get to do this in our own unique ways, and we need many different avenues to receive these insights. I designed my life around these insights rather than letting doubt dictate my actions.

When we do this, we no longer need to prove ourselves; our lives become the proof. Once we are fully embodied, our life becomes a signal. Our boundaries teach; our choices disrupt; our presence recalibrates the atmosphere around us.

You stop convincing others. You stop performing spirituality. You stop translating truth for comfort. You live it. You become unapologetic about who you are. This is how paradigms shift quietly, relationally, and relentlessly.

At one point in my journey, I became incredibly outspoken. I could no longer stay silent just to be nice. I realized that being nice is overrated, but telling the truth, even if it upsets others, is what keeps us true.

I realized that telling the truth and upsetting people was the reason I abandoned myself in the first place. It became clear to me that speaking my truth was what kept me at peace within myself, and that was my priority. This became my barometer for assessing how well my life was going. Things were always working out for me, but that no longer meant having everybody like me. It meant that the people who liked me were more interested in growth than in being agreed with.

Of course, I had to learn to soften my delivery at times, but the truth always needed to be communicated. Holding it in hurt too much, and my body would resist any attempts to stay quiet when I saw things so clearly. The unapologetic way of being is the way of the spiritual warrior.

One of my favorite parts of coaching is when clients gain clarity about their paths, and we practice giving a voice to that clarity. I encourage them to go home and articulate everything they feel out loud, even if it's just to themselves. By empowering our voices, we heal ourselves, making it less important to seek validation from others. We regularly validate ourselves, and over time, this becomes comfortable. When you give yourself a voice and hear it spoken aloud, it carries a different weight. It's crucial to express it.

As I guide clients through this process, they often experience a transitional period. Initially, it feels scary but powerful. This is a time to connect with yourself and your inner divinity. You are hearing your truth and feeling the benefits of clarity more and more. Once that peace is established, you begin to crave alone time while also welcoming the company of others. You no longer feel lonely but are energized by your alone time.

You start to pray to the God within you rather than to false idols. Instead of worrying about the energy surrounding you, you become more natural and neutral, knowing that others' energies will not affect yours. You become less reactive and more emotionally stable. Your concerns about the environment fade because you become the dominant energy in your inner world.

The higher calling often requires disappointing others, letting go of certain identities, releasing imagined futures, and tolerating misunderstandings without defensiveness. It also demands a commitment to reality over fantasy.

Trading Fantasy for Reality

As you become more secure with yourself, you will let go of the fantasies you once lived for. Dropping those fantasies can be challenging; it is not punishment but a process of refinement.

This is your opportunity to create your own genuine fairytale, not a false one. You become fully present in your life and stop trying to escape it. No longer do you seek to belong somewhere, as, when you belong to yourself, you end up feeling like you belong everywhere.

You are meant to stand firm in your own identity. In all environments, you are known, seen, and respected. If you are in places that do not respect you, those places simply aren't meant for you.

This is true even of your family. At one point, I didn't care whether I belonged to my family. We find our soul family. When you emit an authentic spark, others on the authentic path can feel you.

I stepped into a larger purpose and began helping tens of thousands of souls heal and live their best lives. This was when my mission became my focus, and that mission was where I had always belonged.

Valerie

One of my clients, whom I'll call Valerie, is twenty-nine. She came to me because she wanted to feel confident enough to become a famous singer.

Valerie felt that she was destined for more, but she struggled to allow herself to make it happen. She also knew she had spiritual gifts, but those gifts were overshadowed by her coping mechanisms. She developed an eating disorder because she wanted to look a certain way so that people would recognize her as special. However, Valerie would tell me that this eating disorder also served as her excuse for feeling unworthy compared to a healed person. The coping mechanism she created to feel enough was also her excuse to feel less than. This was Valerie's trap to stay small.

Our coping mechanisms start to work against us. They shift from feelings of safety to feelings of imprisonment as we seek to elevate ourselves. One part of Valerie needed to be seen as special, while another part of her used her struggles as a reason for staying small.

Do you see the pattern we create for ourselves? After working with Valerie for a couple of weeks, I suggested that she take a deeper look at her family dynamics. She was operating from an original wound that had become her emotional blueprint. I see this in any client who still, at a cellular level, believes they are the problem.

We needed to shift this for her. I asked if she felt like the family scapegoat, and initially, she said no. She viewed her role as the one who kept everything together, but in reality, she was abandoning herself to avoid being abandoned.

She was doing this through her food issues and by literally trying to shrink herself to fit in with her family. She engaged in these behaviors to remain small, just like them.

As Valerie became more comfortable with me, she decided to dig deeper. She talked to her sister and mother about her childhood, and both said she always had issues with everything. They viewed her as frustrated and angry.

So, I asked her what she was truly angry and frustrated about. She realized that she had internalized her feelings of frustration about not being able to be her authentic self within the family system, but she had never questioned that. She'd never questioned why she had not been allowed to be her fully expressed self at home. She'd felt she had to shrink to fit in, and that was just the way it was.

Her outlet became music, but the issue of upper limits emerged there as well. She moved to a different country to escape and explore her dreams, but her internal coping mechanisms followed her.

It's one thing to leave a toxic environment, but you can't leave the toxicity within yourself. This is why people often say, "Wherever you go, there you are." She was still attracting toxic relationships.

She wondered why she continued to attract those who were clearly unavailable. I explained that it was because she was still partially unavailable to her deepest truth, her inner child. She didn't understand at first, so I broke it down for her.

"Your inner child wants to be allowed to shine, right?" I asked. She nodded in agreement. I then posed a series of questions, encouraging her to respond instinctively rather than overthinking.

"Why don't you shine?" I asked.

"Because it's scary," she replied.

When I probed further, asking what specifically was scary about her shine, she admitted, "I don't know what it would look like."

I questioned her need to see what it looked like, and her response surprised even her: "I need to make sure my family will still love me." I paused, taken aback, and asked why her family wouldn't love her if she changed her role.

She hesitated but then admitted it felt like guilt was surfacing. I encouraged her to give that guilt a voice. Guilt responded, "I can't have more success than them. If I do, it's as if everything they went through was for nothing."

I asked her what this meant to her, and she explained that her family had endured so much and never gotten the chance to shine. "So," she said, "how does it make sense that I get to?"

Another part of her struggle was her sense of capacity. She didn't believe she was capable of achieving success on her own and stayed small just in case she failed. "Why would I deserve more money to take care of myself when I can't even do that now?" she wondered. This was interesting, as it highlighted her upper-limits issue; she couldn't make sense of it within her own belief system.

I suggested that perhaps she was meant to be the cycle breaker. Maybe her shine could heal her family from the unhealed wounds that had prevented them from granting themselves the permission to shine in their own lives.

Valerie admitted that this perspective hadn't crossed her mind, but she still questioned why she felt guilt. Once again, she was allowing negative emotions to define her narrative and shape her truth. I reminded her that guilt often means "I am doing something wrong."

Shame tells us there's something wrong with us. As she began to clear away much of her own shame, she realized that she wasn't wrong; rather, something was off with the family dynamics. This realization gave her a chance to explore her longstanding feelings of shame.

Her shame often made her feel guilty whenever she did anything for herself that didn't also benefit others. We examined her sense of over-responsibility. I asked her why it was her responsibility to ensure everyone else was healed. She admitted that she didn't know. This brought us back to her original childhood blueprint of always having to make sure everything and everyone was okay.

Then she questioned whether it was okay for her to follow her own dreams. I asked her if her loved ones would be justified in rejecting her for being successful, and she quickly replied, "Of course not."

So, I inquired about her thoughts on what she would feel for them if they did reject her during her success. She said, "I just don't want to see them. I don't want to acknowledge that this is how they are." I pointed out that ignoring how they are, while it exists, is actually worse.

"You're gaslighting yourself," I told her. "We can't make people want to be happy for us, but we can choose to be happy for ourselves anyway."

She expressed worry that she would be alone in her career. She had been denying the possible truth that her family wouldn't support her, so instead, she blocked herself from success so that she wouldn't have to find out. "What's the point if my family can't be happy for me?" she lamented. "I don't want the success."

At that moment, it became clear. I posed another question: "Would you truly be alone, or would you be surrounded by other people who aren't your family?" This perspective hit her differently.

"Maybe it's okay to let them be mad at me," she considered. "Maybe it's not my fault that they feel this way." In that instant, fresh insights began to surface. "Wait a minute," she said. "Maybe it was never my fault that they treated me this way in the first place. Could it be that it was their issue all along?"

Often, when we're caught in these inner-child cycles, we try to delay or deny a painful truth. When we do this, we self-blame. However, when we allow ourselves to see a painful truth, we also set ourselves free.

She had been denying her success out of fear that she wouldn't be able to face her family's lack of happiness for her. To avoid that possibility, she'd held herself back.

Valerie was experiencing an ego death as she let go of her guilt. She was also releasing her need to control her food intake. She had been worried that if she didn't manage her eating, her body would change, and she might no longer be seen as special.

I told her she was shedding her old need for certainty. She was also letting go of the role she had played in her family and even with some of her old friends. Ego death is painful because it not only transforms our identity but also forces us to relinquish the ego that kept us safe within toxic systems. It starts to take a back seat, and we begin to allow ourselves to embrace a non-toxic life.

She didn't want to confront the uncertainty regarding her family and was still afraid of the success that might follow. I encouraged her to take it one step at a time: "You can't predict how you'll feel after transitioning to a new position; it's the process of becoming that defines the journey." Instead of worrying about others seeing her as special because of her image, she was about to feel special herself by finally allowing herself to follow her bigger dreams.

Valerie started her YouTube channel because I urged her to share her journey with others. This way, she wouldn't feel trapped by shame or alone in her experience. She discovered that many people resonated with her authenticity.

As she spoke her truth, she reassured her inner child that it was safe to be seen. This act also conveyed to her inner child that she was their biggest supporter, leading her to begin self-partnering.

In this process, we start to reparent ourselves, becoming the caregiver to our inner child that we never had but always needed. The ego begins to fade into the background when there's nothing to prove or protect; instead, only the truth remains to be expressed.

Today, Valerie is working on her record deal and attracting more conscious friendships. She recently shared that she has never felt so safe in herself and feels truly seen by her community. Her journey continues, but she now understands that her success is not solely about her; it's about liberating herself and helping others do the same by being an example of her authentic self. The more authentic she is, the more authentic connections she finds.

By the way, her family has not abandoned her. They live in another country but regularly reach out to hear her updates. Spiritual authority embodies integrity.

Spiritual Authority

Spiritual authority does not announce itself; it emerges as a byproduct of integrating your inner child and aligning your daily actions with the self-worth you now embody. Integrity has a significant impact because people can sense truth and trust it.

This essence is who you were as a child, but you were punished for it. For years, you've been afraid of fully owning yourself and stepping into your power because you experienced rejection when you did. Now you face an upper-limits issue.

You may have sabotaged opportunities when you were close to achieving what you wanted. You did to your inner child what was done to you in your own childhood. Your ego seeks to protect you from rejection and pain, but your higher self knows you need to reclaim your personal power to fully embrace your higher calling.

Inner Child Exercise:

Close your eyes and center yourself. Take deep breaths in through your nose and longer, deeper exhales through your mouth.

This practice allows you to become present, regulate your nervous system naturally, and relax. Focus on your breath: inhale deeply and exhale fully. Imagine yourself in a safe place.

Start by discovering where your safe place is. Is it a location you know, or is it something you've imagined in your mind? Take a moment to notice how it feels.

Is it familiar? Are there pictures in this place? Are you inside or outside? Are there animals present? Allow your mind to create the safe place you need and immerse yourself in it. Continue to breathe, and after a few rounds of breath, I invite you to welcome your inner child to join you.

It's a simple invitation. Even if you don't know what your inner child feels or looks like, or how to connect with them, just trust the process. This inner child is a younger version of yourself.

Invite your inner child to be with you. Take your time and wait until you can see them. If you don't see them right away, don't worry. After years of being sidelined or silenced, they have learned to keep their distance.

They have learned that it's not safe to show up, as they often go ignored. This isn't your fault; it's simply how you've been conditioned to stay safe. But after you've initiated this process for a few days or weeks, they will begin to come forward, I promise.

If you do see your inner child right away, take note of their age. This is the age that needs to be acknowledged. Often, this is the age when you first felt pain or separation from yourself or others. Sometimes, the inner child will present as a version of you that has not yet experienced hurt or confusion.

Ultimately, it doesn't matter what age appears; what is important is that you create a connection. When I facilitate this exercise with clients, I often identify the age for them, but you can learn to do this for yourself.

Observe your inner child's age and mood. Are they trying to hide, or are they eager to connect? What are they wearing? Where are they located? Get as specific as possible about where they are in your space. Again, consider whether this is a place you know or something you've made up. How do you feel about this place? Did your inner child choose it?

Get curious. Once you understand their mood and attire, see if there's any connection. Extend your hand and invite your inner child to come closer. Observe if they resist or if it feels comfortable. Are they eager to join you, or are they neutral?

All of this matters. If they don't come to you, gently ask what they need to feel safe. If they do approach, thank them for their bravery.

Ask them how they're feeling and if there's anything you can do at this moment to make them more comfortable. Follow their requests.

Inquire if there's anything they want you to know right now. Ask them why they decided to come forward now and what happened at that age.

Check if they feel seen by you. If not, ask how you can make them feel more acknowledged and included in your life. Inquire whether they are happy with your current life or if changes are needed. What can you do to facilitate those changes for them?

Ask how they feel about becoming a regular part of your daily routine. Observe their relationship with you. Are they distant, close, familiar, or disconnected?

Take note of their feelings. Ask your inner child if there is a gift you can give them. Tune in and notice what comes to mind as a potential gift. See if there's anything they would like or if there's anything you can do for them at this moment.

Commit to regularly checking in with your inner child. Gauge their reaction to this commitment and, before concluding the session, express gratitude for their presence and convey your excitement about honoring their feelings now. If you feel the need to ask for forgiveness or apologize, do that as well.

After you finish this session, commit to daily acknowledgment of your inner child. While brushing your teeth in the morning, look in the mirror, connect with your eyes, and tell your inner child that you look forward to integrating them into your day.

Throughout the day, take random moments to check in. Ask them what color they would like you to wear. If you receive an answer, make sure to wear that color. Consistently checking in builds trust with your inner child. Listening to them and acting on their wishes makes them feel validated, important, and included in your life.

This relationship dynamic will evolve as they begin to mature, and I'll guide you through that process. When I engaged in deep inner-child work, I noticed that over time I began to refer to my inner child differently. Initially, I called my inner child "it," then "her," and eventually "us." When I knew I had fully integrated my inner child, I simply referred to it as "me."

Observe where you currently stand with this. There is a beautiful integration process that unfolds as you navigate this work, leading to a sense of wholeness in which you no longer feel separate from any part of yourself. You will come to love all parts of yourself, stand up for yourself, and self-partner.

You walk through life as a whole person who understands who you are and why you are that way, and you live accordingly. The level of integration you achieve is reflected in your sense of integrity.

One thing to notice as you engage in this work is that your inner child will begin to mature from those stuck parts. Your inner child will start to grow into your teenage years, and this is when you need to establish boundaries and pay attention to what they are asking for and why. Therefore, it's important to be aware of this process. As you practice these exercises, you will develop deeper self-trust.

As you learn to acknowledge and embrace your inner child, you will also develop the ability to listen to, follow, and integrate their needs. Through this process, you can build not only self-trust but also trust in God, which signifies your higher calling.

Living in such a way that self-betrayal becomes impossible reflects who you have authentically been all along. As a child, you expressed your true self in an environment that did not support that authenticity.

You may have learned to suppress your senses, needs, and abilities, effectively breaking your boundaries. Growing up in an emotionally dark environment can force you to adopt identities assigned to you, such as that of a scapegoat, just to feel attached and safe.

However, as you cultivate your self-trust, you reawaken your original boundaries and reconnect with your true self. The inner critic that once held you back starts to fade, making way for your inner cheerleader to emerge. This marks the reclamation of your true identity.

Many clients share that as they integrate with their inner child, they also revive dreams they once held as children. For instance, one client, who always wanted to be a veterinarian, ended up as a project manager. She felt she wouldn't earn enough money as a vet or might struggle to get hired.

Though she felt disempowered regarding her gifts, she never abandoned that childhood dream. Now, at fifty-nine, she has three cats, two guinea pigs, and two birds. I told her that, in a sense, she is a vet in her own household. Despite feeling too old to become a vet, she is fulfilling the desires of her inner child without even realizing it.

Another client had always wanted to help people but had found herself managing celebrities for the past fifteen years. To her, that translated to helping others achieve fame, but deep down, she wanted to shine herself.

After eight months of working with me, she decided to resign. Her body could no longer endure sidelining her own needs for the sake of others' success. Growing up, her mother had been the star, and she had been there to provide support. Now, though, she was ready for an upgrade. No more issues with upper limits.

I asked her if she had always wanted to help people or if that was simply what she had learned was her value. Had she received love when she'd supported her mother's dreams? The answer was yes, she learned her value through helping, and she also received love when supporting her mother's dreams. But she also had her own dreams. She decided to take a break from managing others and record her own single.

She had always loved singing, but her mother never encouraged it. After recording her first single, fortune smiled upon her. She had already been connected to the music industry through years of managing artists. Now she has her own agent and is on the road, opening for a famous band.

Your purpose cannot bypass you. It evolves as you heal. You may think it has been delayed, but the truth is, you were simply undergoing the lessons you needed to become unbreakable.

Our purpose never abandons us. We can't miss what is meant for us, and life has a way of catching up to us as we heal.

Chapter Summary

- **Healing as Preparation for Purpose:** The chapter emphasizes that healing is not the final goal but the groundwork for living one's higher calling. Sensitive souls are not meant to awaken simply to feel better; they are meant to embody their truth so fully that their lives become a path for others.
- Embodiment Makes the Life the Message: Once a person is integrated, they no longer need to prove, persuade, or perform spirituality. Their boundaries, choices, voice, and presence become the teaching, quietly influencing others through lived integrity rather than explanation.

- **Speaking Truth as Spiritual Authority:** The author reframes truth-telling as essential to self-respect and peace, even when it disappoints or unsettles others. Spiritual authority arises when a person stops abandoning themselves for approval and begins trusting their own voice, inner knowing, and alignment with God.
- **Releasing Fantasy and Choosing Reality:** A major part of stepping into a higher calling is letting go of imagined futures, false identities, and the need to belong in places that do not honor one's truth. As self-belonging deepens, the person no longer chases validation and instead creates an authentic life that naturally draws aligned people and opportunities.
- **Inner-Child Integration as the Foundation of Calling:** The chapter teaches that reclaiming purpose requires building a real relationship with the inner child through daily acknowledgment, trust, and action. As the inner child becomes integrated, the person develops self-partnering, self-trust, stronger boundaries, and a deeper connection to their authentic desires.
- **Purpose Returns as Healing Deepens:** Through Valerie and other client examples, the chapter shows that people often reconnect with the dreams they had suppressed in order to survive their family systems. The core message is that purpose is never truly lost or missed; it waits beneath the wounds, and as healing unfolds, it re-emerges in a form that is stronger, freer, and more aligned than before.

CHAPTER 9

EMBODIMENT: BECOMING THE PROOF

At this point, you no longer ask, *What's wrong with me*? or, *How do I fix this?* Instead, you ask, *What is true, and am I living it?* That question is transformational.

True transformation doesn't look dramatic; it manifests as a healed nervous system. From this place, you naturally make different choices. Once I healed my nervous system, I no longer found excitement in toxic cycles.

Now those same cycles make me cringe. I feel more grounded when I observe something that feels wrong and choose to engage only when it feels right. When old patterns surface, I no longer feel compelled to engage with them.

You, too, are no longer bonded to trauma, either with yourself or with life. This is the point at which you cease to tolerate toxic partners. You stop being toxic to yourself. This is what sovereignty looks like.

Jen

Jen came to me for business coaching, and we worked together for six months. She wanted to increase her income but couldn't understand why her business, which looked good on paper and felt aligned with her, wasn't earning as much as she had hoped.

Jen had transitioned six years ago from nursing to coaching, and she loved what she did. I could see the passion she had for the few clients she had at the time. However, after our first session, it became apparent that she was functioning from a place of scarcity. Each subsequent session, she brought up issues that had little to do with her business and more to do with her anxiety about money and her business's future.

Jen had a completely dysregulated nervous system. As a highly sensitive person, she found it nearly impossible to navigate the world as she had been. Like many of you reading this book, Jen revealed that she often felt she had been born into the wrong family and sometimes even the wrong planet.

Jen had mastered the art of people-pleasing and surrounded herself with friends. She had undergone an ego death and experienced the pain of losing her old friend group when she stopped drinking by choice. By taking alcohol off the table, she forced herself to learn how to regulate herself naturally, and this helped her to no longer numb the pain through people-pleasing. However, she'd recognized that it was time to distance herself from that behavior and many of those relationships.

She felt her current community was supportive and aligned with her values. She had done significant inner work and believed she was exactly where she was meant to be, but this financial aspect of her life was quite perplexing.

In the second month of working with Jen, she began to make significant money. I helped her build and launch her first online course. She went from making $6,000 a month to earning over $20,000, and she was thrilled.

However, that excitement faded when, the following month, her earnings dropped significantly. She was unable to maintain that level of success.

Jen had been relying on her income to feel safe in her body. This moment marked a crucial opportunity for her to discover her true self and redefine her worth independent of her financial situation. I told Jen that money does not heal our wounds; it exposes them. She realized she had not developed the capacity for self-trust and had not honored her ability to energetically hold more in her life. As long as I was there to mirror Jen, she made the money; as soon as she took a month off, she was unable to hold that mirror for herself. She had not yet practiced the frequency of self-support.

I understood that what Jen truly needed was to heal her inner child and recognize that she was not the issue, but rather, her nervous system was. During our conversation, Jen said, "Candace, I don't even want to work so much. What I truly want is a divine partnership."

She longed for safety and desired a partner who would not rescue her from her situation but help her build a more solid foundation. Ultimately, Jen was seeking safety within herself. She was also honest with herself about wanting to be in a partnership as a way to feel supported while she healed. I reminded Jen that we can't hold money if we can't anchor safety.

I found her request to be wise. Jen recognized that she needed to heal herself, but she was also asking for support. It became clear that she had been a scapegoat in her family dynamics.

She received little support from her father, and her relationship with her mother was fraught with conflict. Her siblings were also caught in the middle, and even her extended family distanced itself. Throughout her life, Jen had been labeled as the "different one," leaving her confused about why.

Her need for money was a way of asserting her worthiness, which needed to be addressed. Jen had always excelled in school and performed well in life, but after tuning into her energy, I sensed an underlying wound around jealousy.

I asked Jen if her mother had ever been jealous of her. During our exploration of her inner work, I realized that her mother was not jealous of Jen directly, but rather of the attention Jen received from her father and her siblings.

Jen was a daddy's girl, and her mother exhibited slightly narcissistic tendencies. With Jen's siblings being boys, the dynamic between her mother and them felt less threatening.

Jen's struggle stemmed from her mother scapegoating her because she was female, while her father and brothers favored her. Her mother needed to be the center of attention and exert control, which caused Jen immense pain.

Jen later told me that nothing she had ever heard felt as accurate as this realization, and she was ready to confront this truth. Her mother had created a narrative to separate her from the family.

As she began to process this understanding, memories surfaced that confirmed this family dynamic. Jen had repressed many of these experiences subconsciously as a survival mechanism. This is what often happens: we bury experiences that are too confusing or painful to confront, casting them into the shadows so we do not have to deal with what may be too difficult to process.

We begin to remember our experiences when our nervous system feels safer and more validated. Jen was processing her feelings and, for the first time, felt truly seen. The confusion she had carried for forty years began to clear up. Her situation was no longer confusing; it was clarifying.

As Jen began communicating with her dad, she noticed his resistance to discussing her mother. This indicated to Jen that she was caught in a typical family dynamic where the mother held all the power, while the father went along with the situation. Although her father had always been there for her privately, he didn't provide her with the support she needed within this dynamic; he was just a passive presence, helping her manage life but never protecting or advocating for her.

Jen realized that her tendency to attract emotionally immature or unavailable men stemmed from having a father who lacked backbone and was controlled by her mother. She also recognized that her mother had never prioritized Jen's needs. Jen said to me, "I don't even think my issue is about money. It encompasses everything."

I told Jen that money begins when worth stops being negotiated.

I reassured Jen that her struggle was fundamentally about her capacity to allow herself to have more: "How we do one thing, we do all things." The way we approach one aspect of life reflects how we handle everything. Jen's father would provide her with money only when she was in a dire situation, offering just enough to get by but never more.

We decided to shift the focus from merely making money, as Jen had already demonstrated her ability to do that. Instead, we worked on helping her embody everything she had learned. I told Jen that when worth is conditional, money will be unstable. She needed to establish new boundaries with her family and the men in her life, boundaries that honored her truth and that of her inner child.

Jen was no longer going to accept the minimal attention from her mother or the dismissals from her family. For instance, when she wasn't invited to a family holiday, instead of just accepting it as she was accustomed to doing, she needed to ask, "Why?" She had to start holding her family accountable for their lack of regard for her. Why was everyone so uncomfortable when she was around?

Jen told me that she had always been reprimanded as a child for asking too many questions or reacting to the neglect she experienced. She had been labeled the "problem child" and endured reactive abuse; she was punished for her reactions to the neglect, leading her to learn to stay quiet and distant while suffering the pain of feeling like a stranger in her own family. Jen's nervous system recognized "distance" as "safety." This clarified the reasons for her attraction to emotionally unavailable men. It also explains how she was able to make money but then experience a lack of it.

Within a couple of months, Jen stopped searching for her ideal partner, the perfect place to live, and new clients. She began to relax and recognize the support system she had built around herself. It became clear that she needed to focus on that support and on her strong friendships, which made her feel fortunate.

Jen ceased chasing validation through unstable money flow, unavailable men, and inconsistent clients. Instead, she turned her energy inward and stayed grounded in her current situation. She allowed uncomfortable feelings to surface and worked through them. Jen gave herself the space to come home to herself.

I'm not kidding when I say that two months later, and from out of nowhere, a new man entered her life. This wasn't a chance occurrence; she met him at a friend of a friend's party, not through a dating app. Instead of worrying about how she would meet someone, she met someone in a more aligned way.

Initially, she wasn't attracted to him, but there was something intriguing about him. I encouraged her to slow down and not judge based on initial intensity or chemistry, but rather to get to know him. She appreciated his ability to listen, make her feel centered on dates, and work around her schedule.

He was patient with her, and she began to feel her nervous system expand, allowing her to tolerate this new connection and see it for what it truly was. Within six weeks, she told me she felt the relationship was genuinely good for her, and she also admitted to feeling attracted to him in a different way.

Jen had made a list of fifty qualities she wanted in a partner, and she shared that this man embodied ninety-five percent of them. Now in her forties, she had concerns about her ability to start her own family, but this man had a small child of his own, which caught her attention. Could this be aligned in a deeper way?

Jen stopped worrying about survival. Not only had she learned to embody her boundaries and standards, but she had also learned to let love in. She was expanding her capacity for healthy relationships and growing abundance. Jen began to feel that this relationship was something more spiritual, and day by day, she allowed herself to experience that comfort.

Over the next six months, Jen transformed into a completely different person before my eyes. She radiated happiness that comes only from having a life and a relationship that reflect one's true needs and values. Jen was on her path to becoming a cycle breaker in her family system and a matriarch in her new life with her boyfriend and his young child.

When she took a stand against her old identity, she felt her role evolve. Today, Jen is one of my favorite examples of someone transitioning from survival mode to embodying true love and happiness. The icing on the cake came when she called me to share that she had made significantly more money that year than she had realized.

She hadn't noticed it because she had been too busy exploring her new love and envisioning what that new family dynamic would feel like. That shift from seeking externally to focusing inward is what allowed her to distance herself from draining situations and truly embody her own heart. Jen was no longer the scapegoat. Her original family still has its own work to do, but the win is that Jen no longer takes it personally and no longer feels imprisoned by the old role. Jen is in love, experiencing abundance, living her true reality, and happy!

The final transformation is this: you stop caring about what was never yours, and you embrace a true identity that feels right.

You may not always think of yourself as amazing, but you love all parts of yourself. You no longer absorb the emotional weight of families, partners, systems, or cultures that refuse to evolve. You don't fight against them; you don't try to convince or rescue them. Instead, you outgrow them. You have healed your inner child and no longer seek relationships that mirror your wounds. Instead, you attract relationships that can hold your light.

The last and most vital step in reconnecting with your inner child is to make it a daily practice: the child who was misunderstood, silenced, or punished; the child who learned to hide sensitivity as a survival tactic; the child who believed they were the problem.

Inner-child work is not about reliving trauma; it's about reparenting yourself with compassion. It's a space where your deep sensitivity can be tenderly held and integrated, allowing you to become whole. This happens not by erasing the past, but by embracing it.

An embodied person has integrated all parts of their shadow and their golden shadow: essentially, their shine. They are now regulated. They hold the dominant energy; they possess compassion without self-sacrifice and maintain strong boundaries without feeling guilty. They have depth without dysfunction and live to experience new things.

Mariel

Mariel came to me for an inner-child channeling session. Mariel was eighty, and she told me she had done decades of work. She had seen my appearance on a podcast and had known I could help her with the last piece before it was too late.

She never felt seen and couldn't figure out what was in the way. When I looked into Mariel's energy, I saw a lot of light and also a seven-year-old girl asking for her. As I started my session with Mariel, I had the feeling that she'd never had children. She confirmed that she had been briefly married once but never had children. I told her a seven-year-old was calling to me, and I believed it was her inner child. Immediately, Mariel teared up. She apologized for getting too emotional, and I told her that this is how the work works. The surge of emotion was just soul confirmation.

I took Mariel through an inner-child process. We contacted her inner child, and I asked Mariel what age the child was. She laughed and said, "I see the seven-year-old, too."

As we engaged with her seven-year-old self, there was resistance. I asked Mariel how her inner child felt about me talking with her. The child was excited about that. Mariel told me that the child felt comforted and warm with me. So, I hopped into the space with them.

The seven-year-old Mariel showed me all her younger versions. They were all holding hands, and the seven-year-old was the ringleader. I asked the seven-year-old how she felt about older Mariel. She said she wasn't sure about her and wasn't ready to trust her. I asked her when she felt abandoned by Mariel, and she said, "Now, at age seven."

I had Mariel go back in and ask the child what she needed to be able to trust her. The child said, "More of this." The seven-year-old wanted to be seen by Mariel and acknowledged. Remember, in the beginning, Mariel came to me to help her figure out what her visibility wound was about. The wound was about her not seeing or acknowledging her inner child.

After about twenty more minutes of talking with her inner child, I gave Mariel some homework. She was to contact her inner child daily, listen to any messages it sent, and do whatever the messages suggested.

Two weeks later, Mariel came in for another session. She looked ten years younger. She said, "Candace, she's home." She couldn't believe how quickly this had happened for her. The reason was that she was open, ready, and very compassionate with her little one inside.

Over the course of the next few months, many more memories resurfaced, and Mariel started painting again and wearing more colors. During her first inner-child reading, I'd told her I kept seeing pink and yellow. Mariel had forgotten that, but when I asked her what colors she was drawn to, she said, "I don't know why, because I never liked it, but yellow."

Mariel is now enjoying her eighties, feeling fully expressed, integrated, and happy. It is never too late to heal. It is never too late to live an abundant and happy life. It is never too late to integrate your inner child.

Mariel found her place in the world, and it was with her integrated self. You can also find your way there when you have finally landed in your own heart. Understand that it's not about fitting into this world, but rather about having a mission to heal and to elevate your life.

What this feels like for me is that I wake up every day excited about the life I get to live, the people I can serve, and the mission I share with God. Nothing brings me more happiness than finding my place in the world, the one I created. I know that my partner does not determine my worth; my achievements are simply extensions of my authentic expression, and my voice is now my tool to empower my inner child daily.

Chapter Summary

- **Embodiment as Nervous System Healing:** The chapter defines embodiment as the stage where healing is no longer conceptual but lived through a regulated nervous system. At this point, a person stops participating in toxic cycles, no longer bonds through trauma, and begins making choices from sovereignty rather than survival.

- **Worth Beyond Scarcity and External Proof:** Through Jen's story, the chapter shows that unstable money, relationships, and opportunities often reflect unresolved worth and safety issues rather than a lack of talent. Real abundance begins when worth is no longer negotiated through family approval, financial success, or emotionally unavailable partners.
- **From Survival Mode to Receiving Healthy Love:** As Jen stops chasing validation and turns inward, she becomes available for a calmer, healthier form of love that her old nervous system might once have overlooked. The chapter frames this as a shift from pursuing intensity and scarcity to allowing support, reciprocity, and aligned connection.
- **Inner-Child Work as Daily Reparenting:** A key message is that embodiment requires ongoing inner-child connection, not occasional insight. The misunderstood, silenced child within must be acknowledged, listened to, and integrated daily so that adult life is no longer organized around old pain, fear, or false roles.
- **Integration of Shadow and Golden Shadow:** The embodied person does not merely heal wounds but also reclaims their shine, joy, visibility, and creative life force. This means holding compassion without self-sacrifice, boundaries without guilt, and emotional depth without dysfunction.
- **It is Never Too Late to Become the Proof:** Through Mariel's story, the chapter emphasizes that healing and integration can happen at any age. The final transformation is living as proof that wholeness is possible: no longer seeking to fit into the world, but creating a life that reflects one's truth, purpose, and fully reclaimed heart.

FINAL THOUGHTS

Connecting daily with others on this path of realizing their true purpose has nothing to do with proving yourself or seeking validation; it's about being the truth you were once forced to deny.

You were never misunderstood because you were broken or because there was something wrong with you. You were misunderstood because you possessed a higher consciousness in the family and world into which you were born.

You were misunderstood because you arrived early. You perceived what others could not, and you felt what many avoided.

You carried the burdens that others refused to acknowledge, but now you no longer bear them. You lead, and this is no accident.

This is why you are here. You are not weak, nor are you wrong or deficient.

You were never meant to fit into a mold that could not contain your depth, sensitivity, or so-called flaws and misunderstood truths. These were never liabilities; they were initiating gifts.

These gifts provide the very capacity needed to perceive what others deny and to lead where others cannot yet see. The journey from scapegoat to cycle breaker is not merely about personal healing; it is a sovereign act.

It is the reclamation of your spiritual authority, your inner truth, and the parts of you that were once silenced, shamed, or forced to conform to survive.

When I asked myself, *What if there really is something wrong with me*? I came face-to-face with the old story. I was willing to be that if, in fact, that was my truth. But what I discovered was that the fear of it being true was what was blocking me from the deeper truth. There was nothing wrong with me that I could see, and trust me, I had been searching inward for years.

But then I discovered what was actually wrong. The family system, the societal system, was wrong, and I had taken on the collective shame from those who had conditioned me. When we are afraid of a possible truth, we are also blocked from the absolute truth.

I encourage you to sit with the deepest message, the forbidden truth you fear to be you. This is where wisdom will enter. Anything you fear is just false evidence that appears real because it is still too far away to be seen clearly. Bring it toward you.

As you think about the messages in this book, know that you are already the truth warrior. You took time out of your life to dive into stories that reflect you and those who have had the courage to join you on the path to ultimate liberation. This is how you are setting yourself free. Dare to be anything as long as it is the truth, and the truth will finally reveal itself out loud.

My life has become my teaching, and my story is the curriculum. Today, I live the life I always dreamed of in many ways. But the healing journey does not end; it just continues to expand. I no longer strive for perfection but instead see that the perfection is in the process of becoming more and more of your authentic self.

I encourage my clients to show up messy. Show up just as you are, not the perfect you that you think you would be if you didn't have wounds to heal. Those wounds are the path to your wisdom. They are the perfection of the process. As you embrace these parts of yourself, you will also call in the next level of wisdom. As you stop resisting what is, you open up to what is meant for you.

When I realized that I no longer had to hide my wounds or carry the weight of other people's unhealed trauma, belief systems I did not align with, or fear my individuality, I started to empower the message within me. We are all here to highlight our differences to make a difference. To share our struggles instead of living behind a facade. We are here to be full expressions of the divine within us.

This is not about having a perfect life; that can't exist in such an emotionally dark age. But it is about designing a reality that feels perfect for you. Stop putting achievement, performance, and image on a pedestal. Start prioritizing how life feels to you. This will lead you to an identity upgrade.

This does not require fame, status, or a grand external role, though that can follow if you want it.

Those things are no longer something to validate you, but instead they become an expression of you. What it requires is integrity. When you live as the full expression of your authentic self, regulated, embodied, and emotionally sovereign, you become a stabilizing presence.

Your nervous system becomes the transmission, and your healing becomes the invitation. Without effort, others rise in your presence.

The new consciousness you bring forth does not announce itself loudly. It moves quietly through embodied truth, emotional maturity, and lived wisdom. It doesn't just change your story; it alters what is possible for those who come after you. This is how humanity evolves, one embodied leader at a time.

It took me forever to find my tribe. I ended up creating it. I started sharing my insights and experiences and created my inner circle, which I now call "The Truth Room Membership." This is now an international soul family that I have collected for many years. We meet over Zoom and share in a sacred space of no judgment, total attunement, and, in my opinion, the family most people wish they'd always had. We are a soul family. If this book resonated with you, I encourage you to join. https://candacevandell.com/truth/

The healing journey is not about achieving a perfect life but about creating one that's perfect for you. It's also not about doing it alone. It is about living the authentic life you were born to lead and calling in others who can recognize themselves in you. When you are born too conscious for this world, it also means you are born different to make a difference.

Now is your time to upgrade your own system. Walk in knowing that you came here just as you are with a divine mission to break cycles, upgrade systems, and be a fully embodied, fully expressed, and empowered *you*.

THANK YOU
FOR READING MY BOOK!

Just to say thanks for buying and reading my book. Here are some free resources to help you anchor your next level.

Scan the QR Code:

I appreciate your interest in my book and value your feedback, as it helps me improve future versions. I would appreciate it if you could leave your invaluable review on Amazon.com with your feedback. Thank you!

www.ingramcontent.com/pod-product-compliance
Lightning Source LLC
LaVergne TN
LVHW090605110826
845146LV00001B/268

* 9 7 9 8 9 0 1 5 8 2 1 8 3 *